BOOKS BY SIDNEY HOWARD

THE GHOST OF YANKEE DOODLE

ALIEN CORN

HALF GODS

NED McCOBB'S DAUGHTER
  A Comedy in Three Acts

THE SILVER CORD
  A Comedy in Three Acts

LUCKY SAM McCARVER
  Four Episodes in the Life of a New
  Yorker

THREE FLIGHTS UP
  A Volume of Stories

Published by
CHARLES SCRIBNER'S SONS

THE GHOST OF YANKEE DOODLE

THE GHOST OF
YANKEE DOODLE

A Tragedy

By

SIDNEY HOWARD

CHARLES SCRIBNER'S SONS · NEW YORK

CHARLES SCRIBNER'S SONS · LTD · LONDON

1938

THE CHARACTERS

(In the order in which they appear)

SARA GARRISON, *formerly Sara Fithian, actress. Widow of the late Paul Garrison.*

JOHN GARRISON, *her brother-in-law. Chairman of the Board of the Garrison Tool and Die Company. Aged 45.*

PATIENCE GARRISON, *his daughter. Aged 12.*

MICHAEL GARRISON, *his son. Aged 10.*

THE HONORABLE EDWARD CALLORY, *banker and one-time United States Senator. Aged 75.*

DORIS GARRISON, *John's wife. Aged 37.*

ROGER GARRISON, *Sara's son. Aged 19.*

JOAN GARRISON, *Sara's daughter. Aged 21.*

ROBERT GARRISON, *called "Rudi." John's brother. Publisher and editor of "The Morning Globe." Aged 40.*

MARTIN HOLME, *lately instructor in economics at a California university. Aged 30.*

MARY, *the parlormaid. Aged 28.*

JAMES MADISON CLEVENGER, *newspaper publisher.*

OCKLEFORD, *his secretary. Aged 38.*

STEVE ANDREWS, *his illegitimate son, now serving him as his air pilot. Aged 29.*

BUCK ANSON, *factory superintendent for Garrison Tool and Die. Aged 47.*

A SERGEANT AND TWO MEMBERS OF THE POLICE FORCE.

BURKE, *a reporter. Aged 26.*

DOCTOR MILLER.

The action of the entire play occurs in the library of the home of the late John Garrison, now occupied by his widowed daughter-in-law, Mrs. Paul Garrison. The locale is one of the older Western American cities. The time is eighteen months after the commencement of the next world war.

N.B.: In the original production an intermission of five minutes was placed after the first scene and an intermission of twelve minutes after the fourth scene.

THE SETTING

The library in the Garrison mansion. Christmas morning.

The room stands almost exactly where it stood on the day when the last of Stanford White's decorators placed the finishing touch upon it and found it good. The walnut bookcases have lost none of their walnut solidity, and the tooled Cordoban leather—of both walls and chairs—has lost none of its depth and richness of texture. If carpets or hangings have been replaced, their replacements have been accomplished with truly archeological respect for the past. The room does also present a fairly comprehensive pictorial biography of the late John Garrison, to whose private requirements and idiosyncrasies it was dedicated. Steel engravings, mezzotints and photographs—there is just enough wall space free of books to permit a crowded display—include Thomas Jefferson, Abraham Lincoln (framed with an autograph letter), Grover Cleveland, William Jennings Bryan and Woodrow Wilson (also with autograph); and "The Last Spike" of the transcontinental railroad is being driven in oils over the mantel.

As to furniture, there is a large table desk and some of the chairs are large, too, particularly those with leather backs, and a sofa facing the fireplace is large.

One of the chairs, hereinafter referred to as "Sara's big chair," is placed so that it commands the room with the utmost comfort to its occupant.

As to doors and windows, there is only one group of the latter, and it is built into a bay, and there are two doors and both of them are double, heavy, and handsomely in keeping. One pair gives on the hallway. When this pair stands open it is possible to see, in the hall, a portion of the stair and, beneath the stair, the door to the pantry. The second pair of doors gives on the parlor which, to judge from the glimpse afforded, was done at the same time as the library and in the style of the First Empire.

This visible corner of the parlor should be large enough to show the keyboard of a grand piano, placed against a window, with the right hand properly out.

There must be space in the hall and width on the stair to permit of some considerable playing in that part of the stage. The hall, furthermore, is furnished with a narrow hall table, long enough to take hats and overcoats when required to do so.

This play, produced by the Theatre Guild and first tried out in Rochester and Buffalo, had its formal opening at the Wilbur Theatre in Boston on November 1st, 1937. After two weeks in Boston and a week at the National Theatre in Washington, it opened at the Guild Theatre in New York on November 22nd with the following cast:

SARA GARRISON	*Ethel Barrymore*
JOHN GARRISON	*Frank Conroy*
PATIENCE GARRISON	*Marilyn Erskine*
MICHAEL GARRISON	*Jack Kelly*
SENATOR CALLORY	*George Nash*
DORIS GARRISON	*Kathleen Comegys*
ROGER GARRISON	*John Drew Devereaux*
JOAN GARRISON	*Barbara Robbins*
ROBERT GARRISON	*Eliot Cabot*
MARTIN HOLME	*Richard Carlson*
MARY	*Ethel Intropidi*
JAMES MADISON CLEVENGER	*Dudley Digges*
OCKLEFORD	*Don Costello*
STEVE ANDREWS	*Russell Hardie*
BUCK ANSON	*Donald Black*
A POLICE SERGEANT	*Edward Butler*
POLICEMEN	{ *Arthur Davison* *George Goss*
BURKE	*Lloyd Gough*
DOCTOR MILLER	*Howard Roberts*

The production was directed by John Cromwell.

The setting was designed by Woodman Thompson.

THE FIRST SCENE

The season is observed by a fine Christmas tree—and it is a tree, too, and not one of those evergreen shrubs which serve as trees in city apartments—decorated with much more than oriental splendor. The gifts for an ample and present-giving family are piled beneath, the varied parcels all caparisoned in the gayest accessories of ribbon and cellophane. Fire glows in the fireplace and a heavy snow is falling on the garden out of doors.

> [*Both doors are closed and the room is empty. Silence for a moment. Then, suddenly*]:

JOHN. [*From the front door*]: Merry Christmas, *Sara!*

[*Then voices unintelligible, then*]:

JOAN. [*Nearer*]: Mother! Mother! They've got here!
RUDI. By God if they haven't! Merry Christmas!
SARA. [*She is coming down the unseen stair*]: Merry Christmas, John! Merry Christmas, Doris! *And* Patience! *And* Michael!!

> [*Then a confusion of* VOICES: "*Merry Christmas, Aunt Sara," from the* CHILDREN. "*How did you ever make it?" from* ROGER. "*We did get stuck once or twice!" from* DORIS. "*Take off your things at once!" from* SARA. "*Living in the coun-*

1

try's no joke in this weather!" from JOHN. *Then, clearly*]:

JOHN.   You haven't waited for me?

SARA.   Of course we've waited! Have you had breakfast?

DORIS.   We've had everything, Sara!

MICHAEL.   Everything but our presents!

SARA.   You shall have those at once, Michael. We'll go right in this minute and . . .

JOAN.   We must have a march! A grand march in!

RUDI.   A march? Just you leave that to me! They used to call me "the March King" even before Sousa . . .

[*A piano, from the parlor, now breaks into the refrain of "Over There" played very loudly and very incompetently. A chorus of protests puts an immediate stop to it.*]

VOICES.   Uncle Rudi!

No!

Stop it this minute!

Not that!

That isn't for Christmas!

SARA.   [*Topping them*]: Never mind the piano! We'll sing something and join hands and . . .

ROGER.   You lead the choir, Mother!

[*And* SARA *takes over with "God Rest Ye, Merry Gentlemen." Then, the others joining, she opens the door and the Garrison family circle invades the room.* SARA *first; then, holding her hand,* JOHN; *then, likewise hand in hand,* JOHN's *chil-*

dren, PATIENCE *and* MICHAEL; *then* SENATOR NED CALLORY *and* JOHN's *wife*, DORIS, *and* SARA's *son*, ROGER, *and his sister* JOAN, *and, finally*, RUDI.]

[SARA GARRISON *rejoices in a wise, humorous, human and humane fullness of beauty at its mature height and she exercises her own benign and balanced power, after her own indolent fashion, over all those who enjoy the agreeable experience of her influence. She is alight, now, with the excitement of this Christmas moment and her simple frock becomes her and the room almost equally.*]

[JOHN GARRISON, *the substantial member of the family, is in his late forties, but apart from hair which will turn in spite of conscientious golf and healthful summer holidays, does not look it. His attitude towards life is apt to be easy and philosophical. His mood, at the moment, is serenely happy.*]

[PATIENCE *and* MICHAEL, *the two children, are just two children. Aged twelve and ten respectively, they are neither more attractive nor less objectionable than other children of good family.* SENATOR CALLORY, *at seventy-five, and still every inch the Old Guard Republican, has preserved a wondrously bright eye and prancing step.* DORIS *will always be the Southern belle God meant her to be and a delight to the eye, if not to the mind, in any company. She has retained her hat and fur neckpiece.* ROGER *is a personable young party of nineteen, probably a heart-breaker in the society of his female contemporaries, certainly at his intellectual top on a tennis court. JOAN, his sister, seems at once somewhat more of a person. She is lovely and grave, has her own ideas, and a heart with real depths in it and she is thoroughly at peace with the world she knows because there has never been anything about that world to disturb her peace.*]

[RUDI GARRISON, *some years younger than* JOHN, *has taken less care of himself and worn less well. He is keen, sardonic, lively and, one regrets to say, dissolute. All these things show in a hunted and irritable nervousness which is growing on him. Even his Christmas celebration has about it something cerebral and not wholly stable.*]

[*The Christmas ritual consists in circling the tree to song. Only* JOHN *and* JOAN *do clearly by the words. The others range from passable to frank la-la-la except* DORIS, *who smiles too brightly without making a sound. When the song is ended the circle breaks.*]

MICHAEL.   That's for me! I can tell by the shape.

RUDI.   Shh, kids! Better wait till your Aunt Sara gives the signal.

JOAN.   Always wait for the signal. It's good for your character.

PATIENCE.   Oh, look at all the lovely hair ribbons!

JOHN.   [*Over this chatter*]: There now, Doris! Wasn't that worth the drive in from the country?

DORIS.   You can't give me too much Christmas ritual,

John dear. It's the seamy side I object to. The wear and tear of shopping and . . .

ROGER. What is Christmas anyway, Aunt Doris? It's the festival of the Persian deity Mithra that the early Christians took over to cramp competition in the religion racket. And Christmas trees: what are they? Aboriginal, Teutonic fecundity charms!

RUDI. And that's anthropology A!

JOAN. Somebody crown him with a wreath of holly!

DORIS. Really, Roger! After all the trouble your mother's gone to . . .!

[*But* SARA *is laughing.*]

SARA. Oh, you can't stop me on Christmas, Doris! I love it all: including the seamy side! The year has no climax to it with Christmas left out and the family that can't rise to Christmas is no family worth mentioning! But we must get down to business now.

MICHAEL. Presents?

SARA. In a jiffy, Michael. First we've all got to find ourselves chairs.

[*They proceed, loosely to obey,* DORIS *supervising the* CHILDREN.]

JOHN. While your Aunt Sara reads aloud from the Christmas Carol.

SARA. There'll be no Christmas Carol this year!

[*Sensation.*]

DORIS. Sara!

JOAN. Mother! What's the matter?

ROGER. We love our Christmas Carol! We love our Dickens!

SARA. If you kids hadn't been right about Dickens, I should have left you both on a windy doorstep!

RUDI. My father will rise right up and haunt you if you go changing his Christmas routine on him!

SARA. We're having a Christmas sermon this year instead!

[*General alarm.*]

ROGER. Good Lord, M o t h e r ! Think what you're . . .!

JOHN. A Christmas what?

} [*Together*]

SARA. And Ned Callory's the preacher!

CALLORY. I, Sara?

SARA. You, Ned dear. It came to me trimming the tree last night. Roger and Joan were sticking that Star of Bethlehem there on the top. Those Woolworth stars all want to be comets. This is a solemn anniversary! It's Ned Callory's fiftieth Christmas with the Garrison family!

[*A general spontaneous rising.*]

DORIS. Now isn't that just wonderful!

ROGER. You must be a glutton for punishment, Senator!

JOHN. You're only beginning, you know!

JOAN. That does make this Christmas worth celebrating!

} [*Almost simultaneous*]

RUDI. Pioneers! O Pioneers!

SARA. Don't embarrass him! Let him embarrass us!

[*She sits in her big chair.*]

CALLORY. I'll do what I can, Sara. But I'm blessed if I know how to begin a Christmas sermon!

JOHN. "To be honest, to be kind, to earn a little and to spend a little less . . ."

CALLORY. "O Pioneers" makes a better text for me. Fifty Christmases! Lord! You Garrisons have been generous!

[*A politely deprecatory murmur.*]

There was one of the fifty I came near to missing. '96, that was, the year of McKinley's election.

> [*This to* JOHN *or* RUDI, *and he continues, addressing first one, then another of the company as his ideas turn him from one to another.*]

There I am out in that hall with my arms full of presents, listening to your father's voice. "You can tell Ned Callory we want no full dinner pails in the house this Christmas!"

> [*The laughter of those who have heard this story before.*]

I've told that story before.

RUDI. Can't tell any family anecdote too often.

CALLORY. Well, there never was any sense to this family politically speaking. Why, I've heard Jim Hill go after your father till the sweat came out on Jim's neck and wilted his collar! And old John just grinning there in that chair of Sara's. And the vipers he took to his bosom! Single Taxers, the Populists, the Non-Partisan League! If he'd lived he'd have been a New Dealer sure as sin! How he could reconcile his ideas with the money he made! And the same for you coupon-cutting Socialists these days! Yes, I mean you, Rudi, with your pesky, trouble-fostering, labor-lopsided newspaper . . .

> [*He puts such hate into this last adjective that* RUDI *cannot but bridle.*]

And you, too, John Junior, emasculating your country's manliness with your Unions for Peace, and where have *they* got you?

DORIS.   Good for you, Senator!

> [*Protests from both* BROTHERS.]

CALLORY.   I've affection enough for both of you as men, but I never could understand your carryings-on! The pair of you squandering the wealth your father left to you on the enemies of the system by which you live! Biting the hand that feeds you so you can feed the hand that bites you —that's what I'd call it! Liberalism, you call it, I know! Well, your father's to blame with the example he set you . . .!

> [*Both brothers are up and at him but* SARA *calls a halt.*]

SARA.   Children! Children! I know arguments are the Garrison family's weakness, but let's try to get through Christmas without one!

CALLORY.   What's this got to do with Christmas anyway?

> [*And he resumes*]:

There's another Christmas Day this room won't forget.

Old John's last one on earth. There was a world war then.
There's a world war now. Only we were in that other war.
I remember you two boys coming home from camp. Only
your brother Paul was missing. What was it old John
wrote in his diary? "Three generations of Garrisons at our
tree this morning would have made this the richest Christmas I have ever known if only Paul could have got home
from France." We didn't know then that Paul had been
killed.

> [*A general movement, accentuated by* SARA's *still-
> ness, to indicate that the family could do with
> more tact on the preacher's part.*]

And a fine lot of Christmas cheer my sermon's spreading!
I can't help it! What is Christmas when all's said and
done? It's a day set aside for families to get together and
make sure that joy and grief balance each other. God love
you, Sara, for holding this family together! Could you
find such another gathering this day in England or France
or Germany or Russia, or anywhere on that distracted
continent? A family complete and no single member of it
in peril after eighteen months of war? You paid your
share last time when you lost Paul. A brother taken from
you two, a husband from Sara, and from Sara's children
a father whom Joan can't remember and Roger never
knew. Praying's better than preaching in this house today.
God give us the strength to see our troubles through and
keep this nation and its families safe from this war and
lead the world back into its suitable ways.

JOHN.   [*Low*]: Amen to that, Senator.

CALLORY.   My Christmas sermon! Lord! I've made you
all sad.

SARA. You made us seem important and significant people instead of the thoroughly commonplace American family that we are! I liked that even though there's nothing in it! Who wants to be typical?

[*His reply is a warm hug.*]

JOHN. You said things we all wanted to hear.

RUDI. [*Sourly dry*]: Only we didn't know that till we heard you say 'em.

ROGER. And I think it made a nice change from Tiny Tim.

DORIS. [*Dominating*]: Of course, Senator, I find your patriotic convictions more sympathetic than . . .

[*Almost simultaneous*]

[*But SARA's hand is raised and she restores order.*]

SARA. No! Wait! This *was* a solemn anniversary but the solemn part's over! You kids don't have to hold back any longer now!

[*The CHILDREN rush to the tree.*]

MICHAEL. Oh, boy, do I get what I wanted!

[*DORIS follows to the tree.*]

SARA. I've really been economical this year, John, and done all my grown-up shopping upstairs in the attic! In those old trunks marked "Sara Fithian, Theatre!"

PATIENCE. [*Cutting in*]: That's *my* pile!

DORIS. Children! Don't disgrace me!

SARA.   [*Continuing, to* JOHN]: You'll see when you try looking grateful . . .

[*And she, too, turns to the tree.*]

There's a pile for each!

[MARY, *the parlor maid, enters with the mail and paper.*]

MARY.   They just got round with the paper, due to the snow . . .

JOHN.   Oh, let's see the paper, will you, Mary?

[*She surrenders it to* JOHN, *who opens it, the other men gathering around.*]

MARY.   [*Continuing*]: And the postman got stuck in the snow way down the street, so the mail just came, too.

[JOHN *is immediately struck by something he sees in the paper.*]

SARA.   [*To* MARY]: Just dump it there on the desk.

[MARY *obeys and goes.* SARA *turns to* JOAN.]

Don't you think we might get the maids' presents out to them?

[*And, as* JOAN *bends to gather up the maids' presents*]:

Oh, dear, I've forgotten the fundamentals! Where's my cheque book?

[*She finds it in the desk. To* JOAN]:

Take 'em all out. Tell 'em the cheques are coming.

[JOAN *goes with the maids' gifts, returning presently.*]

JOHN.   [*Intent on the paper*] : What's all this, Rudi?

RUDI.   That? Oh, that's our Christmas cartoon. Got to put something in the paper where the ads used to be!

CALLORY.   [*Inspecting over* JOHN's *shoulder*] : What's it signify?

RUDI.   Well, it's a kind of a Christmas angle on the war. Here are the two teams. Germany, Italy and Japan. And France, England and Russia. Here's the American people. They're hard to draw. That's Santa Claus.

CALLORY.   I recognized him.

JOHN.   What are all those diplomas he's handing out?

RUDI.   Can't you read? The blessings of isolation. Trade at your own risk. The usual crap. This big one's our National Honor. See? It's marked "Keep Me Home." That may be a little subtle.

CALLORY.   Pity Santa Claus wouldn't hand out a few jobs and something to eat!

RUDI.   Now would it be tactful to bring that up at Christmas?

[ROGER *has joined the men.*]

JOHN.   Both your teams seem to be taking the holidays easy.

[*The men concentrate on the news.*]

ROGER.   [*Pointing*] : So the French really did sink that freighter of ours!

RUDI.   The *Farragut*, yes. That came through last night.

CALLORY.   [*Reading*] : "Steamship *Farragut*. Bound for Athens, Greece, with a cargo of spark plugs . . ."

[*And he bursts out*] :

Athens is a neutral port in a neutral nation! It's a damned outrage and if we don't take a stand . . .!

RUDI. Aren't a good many cargoes clearing for Athens these days? Don't a good many stop over in Naples? Say "howdy" to Mussolini and just unload without meaning to? And don't the British and French know . . .?

CALLORY. An American ship's an American ship!

RUDI. And contraband's contraband!

CALLORY. And trade's trade!

JOHN. We trade at our own risk in this war, Senator!

CALLORY. But I'm blest if I see why we can't trade in spark plugs! They're not munitions of war!

RUDI. Neither is cotton cloth. But cotton makes uniforms and you can't run a munitions truck without spark plugs, can you? Foreign trade's a fine thing, I know, and business can't do without it, but we're not taking chances on war just to earn money for you business men and . . .

CALLORY. How many American flags have they sent to the bottom? How many young American sailor boys . . .!

RUDI. We're not bringing that up on Christmas either.

SARA. [*From the depths of her cheque book*]: Children!

CALLORY. Neutrality!

JOHN. That's it, Senator!

> [*And he explains himself with complete good humor.*]

We're not satisfied with the way things are going, either. We're not just Christian pacifists, you know. Till the nations can learn how to behave themselves, though, neutrality's cheaper than any alternative. As somebody said: Life is the only wealth.

ROGER.   John Ruskin said it.

CALLORY.   He was a liberal, too. And he lived on the proceeds of the liquor business!

RUDI.   Liberals! You hate the breed, don't you, Senator?

[*He takes* CALLORY'*s arm.*]

You haven't made your annual eggnog yet.

[*They go into the pantry.*]

JOHN.   Sit down, Roger. I haven't had a good look at you since you got home.

[*They sit.*]

How are you boys taking this war back at Harvard?

ROGER.   We take it or leave it alone. You know, Uncle John.

JOHN.   No, I don't know! First year of the last war was my last at law school. Heard nothing but war talk around Harvard then. Boys running off to put on uniforms and drive ambulances and . . .

ROGER.   Didn't you know that undergraduates are more enlightened now than they were in your day?

JOHN.   I'm delighted to hear it.

ROGER.   Oh, they are! We give the question a lot of time and thought. And I'll tell you what we've concluded, Uncle John. This isn't like your war.

JOHN.   My war?

ROGER.   You know what I mean. No martyred Belgium

or *Lusitania* this time. They were great stuff! Made you boys want to fight!

[*But he sees a dangerous glint in his Uncle's eye and quickly remembers to speak his piece.*]

Oh, I know! What did we get out of it but Allies' debts and the soldiers' bonus! And this war's between Hitler and Karl Marx and those of us who've no use for either of 'em hope it ends with both of 'em out of business, and let's us, for God's sake, stay clear of it! I agree with you, Uncle John! That's how the rest of the country feels too, I expect.

JOHN. I hope it is. I believe it is.

[*But* ROGER *cannot quite control natural emotions.*]

ROGER. This ship *Farragut*, though! She's the seventh they've sunk since college began! I've counted, Uncle John!

JOHN. Only you can't say "they," Rog. The Germans got the last one. And the British the one before that and the Japs and Italians . . .

ROGER. I wish the French hadn't got the *Farragut!* I wish it didn't ever have to be France or England!

[JOHN *himself is not as immune as he would like to be.*]

JOHN. So do I, Rog. So do I. But war's war. And we have to watch our sympathies. Because our real responsibility's keeping this country out. I thank God France and England are holding their own. If they weren't it might be harder to keep out.

ROGER. [*A bit wistful*]: And you think it would be wrong to go over and drive ambulances again, with the real will to peace that this country's got?

JOHN.   The *will* to peace. That's the main thing, Rog!

[DORIS, *overhearing, has drawn near.*]

DORIS.   Isn't it just too awful for John to have a patriot wife, who just hates hearing him talk that way to a young boy and he knows I hate it and if he'd only get over this idea of being his brother's keeper . . .

SARA.   People who use that quotation, Doris, never seem to remember that Cain had just murdered Abel when he said it.

[*She rises, handing her cheques to* JOAN, *who takes them out.*]

DORIS.   John knows what I mean and Roger does, too, and coming as I do from a whole family of Confederate Veterans, it just makes my blood boil to see France and England fighting democracy's battle! They're France and England! Oh, I know you're going to throw Russia at me because she's fighting with them! I can't help that! I remember Kitchener's Mob and the old Lafayette Escadrille, so I'm willing to overlook Russia!

JOHN.   Do you want us to fight the French? They just sank the *Farragut!*

DORIS.   They wouldn't have sunk her if we'd been in on their side!

JOHN.   Oh, Doris!

DORIS.   They're our old allies!

[*Her eyes blaze defiance. But* CALLORY *enters from the pantry at this moment carrying a tray covered with eggnog cups.*]

CALLORY.   It's a beautiful eggnog, Sara!

[RUDI *follows him in, carrying the bowl.*]

RUDI. Oh, it's perfection! Where do you want me to put it before I drop it?

SARA. Don't you think it might be less crowded in the parlor?

> [RUDI *is carrying his burden across to the parlor door.*]

We want some perspective on it.

RUDI. She's slipping! She's slipping! Lend a hand with a table, John!

> [JOHN *hastens into the parlor, re-appearing at once with a small table which he places just inside the door.* RUDI *sets the bowl upon it and* CALLORY *the tray of cups.* ROGER *would go to help but* DORIS *takes his arm.*]

DORIS. I recall so well the day my father took his regiment to France in the last war . . .

> [*Her voice rises to hold* ROGER's *attention.*]

"That nation," he said, "that nation which lets slip . . ."

> [*But she must defer to* SARA *at this point.*]

JOHN. There!

RUDI. Thank God.

> [*As the bowl is settled*]:

Now, Sara . . .

> [*He is filling cups.*]

I shall . . .

SARA. You don't think it's too early to start drinking eggnog?

CALLORY. How could it be?

SARA. Well, you know how you feel when you start too early!

[*But none of the men remembers feeling badly.*]

[DORIS *takes advantage of the silence around the punch bowl.*]

". . . lets slip its opportunity to make the supreme sacrifice for its honor . . ."

The most awful condition sets in about three in the afternoon!

ROGER. Wouldn't you like some eggnog, Aunt Doris?

CALLORY. It's nothing! I've had it for years!

[*The eggnog is tasted and approved with a long "AHHH!"*]

DORIS. [*Forte and furious*]: No! I would not!

[*Sensation.*]

CALLORY.   God bless my soul!

DORIS.   What's the use of my being in this house at all if nobody listens to what I've got to say?

SARA.   Doris, I'm sorry.

[*She comes back into the library.*]

DORIS.   I was saying something to Roger for Roger's good!

[ROGER *backs away, frightened.*]

But it doesn't agree with what you Garrisons think and you never listen to any one but yourselves!

JOHN.   Doris, please!

DORIS.   Oh, you can take Sara's side but you know it's the truth!

SARA   [*Low to* ROGER]: Get the kids out, can you?

[ROGER *proceeds to move* PATIENCE *and* MICHAEL —*with presents—into the parlor. As part of this transfer, phrases are dimly audible:* "Come on, kids, into the parlor." "Why?" "Don't you like wrecking parlors?" *But* DORIS *continues over them.*]

DORIS.   [*To* SARA]: Sometimes I wish your Garrison Tool and Die Works would just blow up!

[*Then, at* JOHN]:

So you wouldn't be able to afford to waste all your time on stupid old meetings for peace and committees for civil liberties, whatever they are!

[*And she switches to* RUDI]:

And so you'd have to get out a nice successful paper that

decent people could read without being upset! What good does all your fussing and fuming do?

RUDI. [*Dismayed good humor*]: I wish I could tell you, Doris, but I can't.

[*And to the others*]:

Doris has the might of numbers on her side so she can afford to be magnanimous to us. You know what the giant said when his wife beat him: "It amuses her," he said, "and it doesn't hurt me, so why not?" You're all right, Doris!

[*His arm goes around her waist in spite of her irritable resistance.*]

And I'm going to give you a special Christmas present of a subscription to Mr. James Madison Clevenger's *Morning Eagle*, which ought to be hundred per cent enough even for you!

CALLORY. Hundred per cent or not, Mr. Clevenger's *Eagle* pays its own way, Rudi.

JOHN. [*To* ROGER]: This time we're really off!

SARA. [*A low protest*]: Please! Please!

[RUDI's *smile continues, but his teeth are bare.*]

RUDI. Oh, she'll have the best of the bargain, Senator! Mr. Clevenger's *Eagle's* a much better paper than mine, with lovely features I couldn't dream of affording, because Mr. Clevenger gets out so many papers in so many towns and I've only got my own here!

DORIS. I accept your offer, Rudi! I shall enjoy . . .

ROGER. Aunt Doris! Why, we don't even let the cook take the *Eagle!*

RUDI.   That doesn't matter, Rog. The Senator takes it!
CALLORY.   Yes, Rudi, I do!
RUDI.   I knew it!

[JOHN *is laughing.*]

SARA.   [*A wail*]: Children! Christmas!
CALLORY.   Because Mr. Clevenger's papers remain the last bulwark we conservatives have against you so-called . . .
RUDI.   Oh, there's no name too low for the *Eagle* to call the Garrison brothers! Why, if she believes the *Eagle*—and she will believe it—we feed on the flesh of Democracy's daughters that we roast over fires of burning Constitutions!

[*And he swings savagely on the* SENATOR]:

You think it isn't pretty of me to run a liberal newspaper on what I get from a conservative business! Maybe you know how to make enlightenment pay in the world we live in! We're going to start Christmas over at this point. Go out and come in again on a new foot. Roger, take your Aunt Doris in to the eggnog and get her stinking.

[*General delighted relief.*]

DORIS.   I don't see what I've said to provoke . . .

[ROGER *is already pushing her towards the parlor door. But* MARTIN HOLME—*hat and overcoat—appears in the hall. He is a serious, stocky, sensitive young man of thirty, careless about his dress, travel-worn at the moment, easily at home in the present company.*]

MARTIN.   Merry Christmas. May I come in?

SARA. Martin!

JOHN. Well, if it isn't the professor!

RUDI. It can't be!

ROGER. It is!

SARA. I don't believe it! I don't believe it!

[Almost simultaneous]

MARTIN. It's true.

> *[He enters the room to kiss SARA's proffered cheek.]*

SARA. You can't have come all the way from Los Angeles?

MARTIN. Well, I started from there and I'm here now . . .

SARA. Joan! Where are you, Joan? Here's your young man come home!

> *[JOAN returns from the pantry.]*

JOAN. Martin! Dear Martin!

> *[She is folded in his arms.]*

MARTIN. Glad to see me?

JOAN. Yes, very!

MARTIN. Good! I'm glad to see you.

RUDI. *[Handshake]*: You must be feeling rich.

MARTIN. Not so rich as reckless.

ROGER. Fly?

MARTIN. No. Train. Eight hours late. Snow.

> *[And he is shaking JOHN's hand.]*

ROGER. That's not so reckless. You should have flown.

MARTIN. I wanted to think. Can't think in aeroplanes. Now I'm here I feel giddy.

JOHN. Well, well. . . .

[*He seats him on the sofa.*]

Rog! Get this man some eggnog!

MARTIN. On an empty stomach? I forgot about break-fast this morning.

[*They are all around him.* JOAN *sits on the sofa beside him.*]

JOHN. If thinking ruins your appetite you'd better give up the academic life.

MARTIN. I have.

[*The family stops astonished, but he goes quickly on.*]

And I forgot to wire I was coming. Forgot everything but just getting here. Well, it's all as it should be. There's Senator Callory! Merry Christmas, Senator.

RUDI. You remember Joan's young man, Senator?

[*He does. But* SARA *and* JOAN *are both looking closely at* MARTIN.]

JOAN. You haven't been ill, have you, Martin?

MARTIN. Ill? No. Why?

SARA. Well, aren't you in just a bit of a state or something?

MARTIN. You don't know how it feels to escape from Los Angeles.

SARA. Oh, don't I?

JOHN. What did you mean, though, by saying you'd given up the academic life?

MARTIN. Just that. Aren't you glad you won't have to be a professor's wife, Joan?

JOAN.   [*Bewildered*]: Well, I don't know.

[*A general exchange of glances, then*]:

SARA.   When did you reach this decision, Martin?

MARTIN.   It couldn't have been very long after they fired me.

[*Sensation.*]

JOAN.   Who fired you?

MARTIN.   The University did the actual firing.

[*He is on his feet again and moving about uncomfortably.*]

Now, I didn't want that to sound solemn. That's what I've been thinking hardest about. How to make it sound casual, you know, and . . .

SARA.   But they couldn't have fired you!

MARTIN.   They did. They bounced me right out on my ear.

JOAN.   Just like that?

RUDI.   What for?

MARTIN.   It's so hard to say without sounding solemn.

[*He stops himself in distressful embarrassment, then*]:

But I just don't know how to teach present-day economics without some mention of the late Karl Marx. So I came right out and spoke that four-letter word to a lot of our American boys and girls. And that was enough. Now John Haynes Holmes and Rabbi Wise'll hear about it and . . .

[*He shudders.*]

JOHN.   Do you mean to tell me that a University . . .

RUDI.   Well, a Los Angeles University . . .

ROGER.   That wouldn't have happened at Harvard.

[*Together*]

[SARA *sits.*]

MARTIN.   Oh, you can't blame the University! After all, when the Clevenger papers get after a man . . .

RUDI.   What's that?

ROGER.   The Clevenger papers!

JOHN.   It isn't true!

MARTIN.   Get this last month's file of his *Los Angeles Eagle* if you don't believe me and see what a beating Mr. Clevenger gave me! They had to fire me! They couldn't do any less! Don't let it spoil Christmas, though. I came here to get cheered up.

RUDI.   You haven't spoiled Christmas for me! I'll cheer you up! Come into the parlor and I'll give you an eggnog bath!

[*He goes into the parlor. The others, except* SARA *and* CALLORY, *are following him.*]

JOHN.   Of course it's quite characteristic of Clevenger . . .

DORIS.   I'm sorry for Martin! But I don't see why he had to teach such . . .

ROGER.   Wouldn't he like some solid food with his eggnog?

[*The voices die out in the parlor.* JOAN *has linked her arm through* MARTIN'S.]

JOAN.   All the presents we sent out to you! You never got them!

[MARTIN *looks at her.*]

MARTIN.   I'm spending Christmas with you. That's enough for me.

[*She smiles up at him. Then, as they begin walking*]:

How does your Christmas thing of Milton's go? You know . . .?

[*She remembers.*]

JOAN.   "The shepherds on the lawn
                Or e'er the point of dawn
                    Sat simply chatting in a rustic row . . ."
MARTIN.   I get you . . .
"Perhaps their loves or else their sheep
  Was all that did their silly thoughts so busy keep . . ."
It's the ending I like, though.
JOAN.   "But, see, the Virgin blest
                Hath laid her Babe to rest . . .
                And all about the courtly stable
                Bright harnessed angels sit in order service-
                able."

[*They have gone into the parlor.*]

SARA.   Families are work. They're like farms. You have to work 'em to keep 'em.

CALLORY.   The family's a mirror. One of those old-fashioned, bulls-eye, convex mirrors that reflects a whole room reduced and concentrated. You can see all civilization in the family. You can see what's wrong with the world.

[*She smiles. Her hands go out to him. Then*]:

I love you, Sara.

[*He bends over her hands in the most courtly fashion.*]

SARA.   You can't leave without your present from me.
CALLORY.   Do I get a present from you?
SARA.   You get a walking stick.

[*She has gone to the Christmas tree for a silver-capped walking stick.*]

Not that you haven't fifty others already, but this one's rather special. Because it's descended from Paul's and my honeymoon in the Southwest, from the desert and sandstone and the wide, dry rivers Paul loved, from an Indian pueblo where the Chief was a friend of Paul's, and this was his wand of office from Abraham Lincoln. You can see the signature "A. Lincoln," engraved here on the top. And that's because, back in the Civil War—families were splitting on an issue then—the Confederates tried making Indian trouble for Lincoln. And Lincoln sent these walking sticks, one to each chief, like a feudal king swearing vassals to loyalty. And the tribes didn't make trouble and the chiefs still hand their staffs on to their successors. . . . One day, long after Paul's death, this came through the mail. There weren't any more Indians left in that pueblo. I like to think that Lincoln would have given the Indians a more generous deal than the Senators of your generation gave them, dear Ned.

[*She holds the walking stick out to him.*]

CALLORY.   [*Much moved*]: Are you sure you want me to have this?

[*She smiles.*]

SARA.   It's pioneer stock! It's old American!

CALLORY.   If I'd had it in time it would have walked me straight into the White House!

SARA.   In whose place?

CALLORY.   Harding's. Thank you and God bless you, Sara.

[*He goes into the hall.* JOHN *and* RUDI *have appeared at the eggnog bowl.*]

SARA.   Now I'm started on this . . .

[*She turns back to the Christmas tree for two more parcels, one a book, the other a framed picture.*]

John, my dear brother-in-law, and much better than any brother I've known about, will you accept this treasure I'd forgotten I owned? It's the very rare, very first edition of *Huckleberry Finn*, with the accidentally dirty picture in it that got it suppressed when it first came out, and that makes it what's called a collector's item, though I can't find any picture we'd call dirty now! Your father gave it to me my first Christmas here. To make up for the row he raised when Paul married an actress. I'd told him how Mark Twain wanted me to play Joan of Arc, and you know how your father worshipped Mark Twain.

[*But* JOHN *is unaccountably troubled.*]

JOHN.   You shouldn't be giving your treasures away now, Sara!

SARA. But I believe in passing the past along and making it somebody else's future!

[*Then, to* RUDI]:

I want you, Rudi, as the companion of my baser nature—don't misunderstand me, John, will you?—to have George Bellows' report on the immortal wallop Firpo handed Dempsey. I used to creep round with this print at night and hold it up to the walls and say to myself: "My God, what a sock that was!" But these walls never seemed to do Bellows justice! Here it is, Rudi dear, in memory of the journey we made to see Schmeling knock out Joe Louis.

[*She is suddenly angry.*]

And how he knocked him out! And how he should have had his crack at Braddock!

[*Then*]:

Come in here, Joan, and get your Christmas present!

[JOAN *enters to meet the large box her mother is holding out to her.*]

JOAN. From you, Mother?
SARA. Oh, very much from me!

[JOAN *drops on her knees where she stands to tear the box open.*]

From the very gizzard of the old theatre trunk in the attic!

JOAN. [*Pointing to the label*]: From Jaeckel!
SARA. It came from Jaeckel a great many years ago, and it's just been back there having its face lifted.

[JOAN *sits back on her heels to display a most beautiful evening coat of ermine.*]

JOAN. Mother!

SARA. I don't want to be thanked! I've never felt right about that piece of goods. A man gave it to me once as the price of my virtue. I kept the virtue but didn't send back the coat. Let's see if it suits you.

[JOAN *is on her feet and into the coat.*]

Yes, I think it does. It makes you look less like a lover of poetry. Now, go dazzle Martin and Rog.

JOAN. [*She runs into the parlor, calling*]: Martin! Rog! Aunt Doris! Look at what mother's given me for . . .

[*Confused exclamations from those called upon.*]

DORIS. [*Off-stage*]: Joan, how beautiful!

JOAN. [*Off-stage*]: Mother gave it to me! It's an old one of hers made over!

ROGER. [*Off-stage*]: Let's go right out to a party! I wouldn't mind taking my sister out in that!

MARTIN. [*Off-stage*]: It's not ermine, is it?

SARA. I like my daughter, if she is a bit serious. I like Martin, too, and they'll live a perfectly rapturous life together, never seeing the funny side of anything.

[*She is back in her big chair again.*]

Only we've got to pull the boy over this brutal deal Mr. Clevenger's given him. We can't just leave him to join the persecuted professor's club. Bring me some eggnog, Rudi, and we'll think what to do.

[RUDI *fills two cups of eggnog at the bowl.*]

Martin needs two things: a wife and a job. The wife's all fixed. [RUDI *delivers one cup to* SARA *and offers the other to* JOHN. JOHN *refuses.* RUDI *sits, sipping it himself.*]

And there shouldn't be any trouble about the job. One has to find room for family in a family business. What else is a family business for except to live on?

JOHN.   Oh, I see your point, Sara.

SARA.   [*To Rudi*]: I'm not getting the encouragement I expected. Rudi, you'll have to make room for him on the *Globe*. And I'll build them a little home. Out in one of those new "developments" where young couples start life in old English bird houses. House, lot and furniture: what should that come to, John? Don't scream, I shan't need it all at once.

[JOHN's *reaction to this is mournfully humorous.*]

JOHN.   The question isn't getting it all at once. Do you get it at all?

SARA.   Now, John!

JOHN.   The concept of free will, Sara, has been fun to philosophers for centuries and in times of peace we're allowed to enjoy the illusion.

SARA.   Where's your toga, John? Don't tell me it's gone to the wash?

JOHN.   [*Good humor unshaken*]: You *are* reckoning without Hitler and Mussolini, Sara. And now that those two paranoiac playboys have seen fit to wash the world in blood for despair of their prestige as dictators, all of these private things that mean so much to us and so little to any one else are conditioned . . .

[*Now* SARA *is really vexed.*]

SARA.   Oh, it's too bad of you on Christmas, John! I won't listen!

[*She rises.*]

I won't listen!

JOHN.   You've got to listen.

[*She turns annoyed.*]

I'd intended keeping my counsel till Christmas was over. I know you, once you get an idea, though. And I know how Rudi always aids and abets you. So I'm compelled to put a simple choice up to you both. Between saving our extremely serviceable family business and letting it go to the wall. If it does that, of course, your plans haven't much chance of . . .

[RUDI *is on his feet, thunderstruck.*]

RUDI.   Holy God!

JOHN.   There's nothing so startling in that possibility these days, is there? After all, Garrison Tool and Die's no . . .

[SARA *sits, deeply shocked.*]

SARA.   But you can't let it go to the wall! It's your father's business that he built up and left to you to look after!

JOHN.   This neutrality's turned out more costly than we expected. Even those of us who are most whole-heartedly for it. A good many concerns have collapsed in the eighteen months since this war began. In the last week two of our most valued customers. Both of 'em leaving large, undelivered orders for us to dispose of. And yesterday, while we were still groggy from that blow, a third valued customer cancelled a third large order, with the friendly advice to sue if we want to and good luck to our suit. We needed those three, because we haven't any others worth mentioning. And because we happen to have a note coming due the 15th of January. A big note, for a modest company. With interest, seven hundred and thirty odd thousand dollars. The prospects of meeting it are a bit complicated.

[*A pause, then suddenly a burst of laughter from the parlor and, on* SARA's *signal,* RUDI *closes the parlor doors.*]

SARA. You have to go very slowly and be very clear when you're talking business with me, John.

RUDI. Strikes me you've had your nerve to keep this to yourself!

JOHN. It's all happened pretty fast. You fight fans might call me a trifle punch-drunk.

SARA. What's it likely to mean?

RUDI. That we'll be in receivers' hands ourselves in about three weeks!

[JOHN *maintains his smiling calm.*]

JOHN. It's true that we've no funds. It's true that our creditors won't give us any more time . . .

[*But* SARA *laughs at this idea.*]

SARA. How ridiculous, John! Creditors always give time! Do you think an old actress doesn't know about creditors?

JOHN. My dear Sara, these aren't the type of creditors you remember. They're the Pioneer National Bank.

SARA. That's Ned Callory's bank!

RUDI. That won't make any difference.

SARA. Don't be silly! You let me talk to Ned and . . .

JOHN.   [*Quickly*]: That you mustn't do, Sara! I'm sorry, but you really mustn't.

RUDI.   It would only embarrass the Senator.

SARA.   But he was here, singing around our tree this morning!

[*Then*]:

Did he know all the time that we . . . that he . . .?

JOHN.   I expect he wanted to spare Christmas, too.

RUDI.   Holy God!

[*He sits again. A pause, then*]:

SARA.   There was a time—wasn't there?—when the state of the world was something to read about and discuss in the village tavern? And when wars came, countries really could keep to themselves and families were secure to go their ways? Or was there ever such a time? Was that just another of our ancestors' delusions?

JOHN.   I'm not as desperate as I might be. And that's because . . .

[*A deep breath, then*]:

Because the Italian Government's prepared to take these cancelled orders off our hands. For considerably more than we should have realized on the original contracts.

[RUDI *looks up sharply.*]

We seem to have made precisely what they need.

[RUDI *is on his feet again.*]

RUDI.   Well, I'll be goddamned! You, chasing war profits! You, with your convictions!

[JOHN *winces but manages to maintain self-control.*]

John. [*Crescendo*]: What else can I do with no orders at home?

Rudi. What else? Anything else!

John. Shut down? Throw the men out of work? When you've got a business to run, you can't let go your hold on it! It won't let go its hold on you!

Rudi. But we're not permitted to sell our wares to belligerents! They're contraband!

[John *is really uncomfortable over what he has next to say.*]

John. It appears the legal side can be got 'round. The sale would be made to some Greek or Guatemalan or other irreproachable neutral in New York and the shipment cleared for some irreproachable neutral port . . .

Rudi. Oho! Another *Farragut!*

John. If the ship's destination's changed later by radio, we've nothing to do with that.

Rudi. Nothing except some pretty cagey conniving!

Sara. Rudi!

[*But* John *strikes back at last.*]

John. I've kept Sara's house and your *Globe* going through these bad times without laying off a single man or cutting a penny of union wages! I knew last summer we'd have to come to this, though I've held off till I couldn't borrow another dime, praying those armies in Europe would mutiny or their peoples revolt! Well, they haven't done either and I can't hold off any longer! There's your choice! Between salvation at a price we hate like hell to pay and shutting up shop!

[Sara *rises suddenly and he breaks off.*]

There are firms with nerve that have taken the chance already. It's just one of the penalties of property, that's all.

RUDI.   If you're not ashamed of yourself, I'm ashamed for you!

JOHN.   I've learned an important lesson these last four days: that we liberals have to live in two opposite worlds. Our beliefs in one, our experience in the other.

RUDI.   That sentiment sounds like an *Eagle* editorial signed by Clevenger himself.

JOHN.   So? Well, speaking of newspapers, you have to think of how you'll feel about giving up the income that pays *The Globe's* deficits.

[*This scores a hit on* RUDI.]

As for Sara's plans and responsibilities . . .

SARA.   You can't hide behind me! I won't have that! I vote no. And without the slightest hesitation. I won't build that house for Joan! They can move in here! It'll be much better than living in an apartment and going to bed in an elevator!

JOHN.   Try to understand, Sara.

SARA.   Is there more?

JOHN.   You won't have any income at all. Not a penny. There won't be any more business. You'll be absolutely cleaned out. So will Joan and Roger. It's the end of everything. Including this house.

[*A pause, then*]:

SARA.   I've loved this house.

[*Her head turns slowly as her eyes range the room.*]

RUDI. [*Almost to himself*]: Because we obey the law and live up to our principles . . .

[*And he turns to* SARA *in a plea almost of despair.*]

But self-preservation! That's a kind of principle, too! What's anything but a compromise with what should be? Father bought me *The Globe!* I've made it the best liberal paper in the country! I can't let it go!

JOHN. You don't have to apologize, Rudi. I've got my old law practice to fall back on so I'm the one with the least to lose. Whereas you and Sara . . .

[*But* SARA *shakes her head.*]

SARA. They must have had some reason for making deals like this Italian thing illegal. I can only see how we'd feel if any deal of ours were to involve this peaceful country in war—I don't know how. I can only see that I've a son just at the fighting age whose father was killed in the last war.

[*She smiles.*]

This isn't the first time I've seen notice put up on the call board.

RUDI. She's perfectly right, of course.

[JOHN *heaves a sigh of relief.*]

JOHN. Thank God she is.

SARA. I mean to see Christmas through now if it kills me.

[*She turns back towards the parlor doors.*]

So I'll ask you not to speak about this to the others.

Just for today. January 15th, you said? Well, there's oil enough to keep the oil burner going!

[*She throws open the door.*]

I need a great deal more of that good eggnog!

> [*But* JOAN, *still in her ermine wrap, enters quickly and tensely, followed at once by* MARTIN, *in the same mood.*]

There isn't anything else the matter?

[MARY, *the parlor maid, enters.*]

JOAN.   Mr. Clevenger's here to see you, Mother.

[*This is a real sensation.* ROGER *and* DORIS *enter.*]

RUDI.   Who? ! ! !

SARA.   Did you say Mr. Clevenger, Joan?

MARY.   Mr. James Madison Clevenger. I'm to say that he's come to wish you a Merry Christmas. You in particular, Mrs. Garrison.

ROGER.   He's waiting in the hall.

RUDI.   But what on earth's he doing in this town? The papers had him in Palm Beach for Christmas!

JOHN.   What's he want with us? You ever meet him, Rudi?

RUDI.   No! Nor do I feel the least desire to!

SARA.   Mary, ask Mr. Clevenger to come in.

JOAN.   Mother! . . . Just a minute, Mary! . . . Mother, you can't let that man into this house!

SARA.   He seems to have got in already!

JOAN.   Then send him word he's not welcome!

SARA.   Please, Joan! He'll hear you!

JOAN.   After what he's done to Martin, I want him to hear!

MARTIN.   I never expected to meet him in this house!

RUDI.   I'll be damned if I stay in the same room with him!

SARA.   Rudi, please! Mr. Clevenger's coming in, of course. I hope we can keep him for lunch. After lunch is over, if it seems worth while, I'll throw him to the lions.

DORIS.   *You* don't know Mr. Clevenger, do you, Sara?

SARA.   Well, it's been a long time, but he still seems to feel some claim on my friendship. After all, he did give me an ermine coat.

[*And she goes out into the parlor, calling*]:

Where are you, Jim? Let's see you! Are you looking older?

[*The others stare after her, stunned, as the curtain falls.*]

THE SECOND SCENE

The room has been cleared of its Christmas litter. Only the tree remains to maintain the atmosphere. The fire glows in the grate. The snow is still falling. It is the afternoon of the same day. The doors to both hall and parlor are closed.

[MR. JAMES MADISON CLEVENGER *sits on the sofa submitting to a massage treatment for stiff neck. He is impressive and impudent, with an ample supply of romantic allure still at his disposal. His secretary,* OCKLEFORD, *who administers the massage, is a bright-eyed bruiser of forty, a bit of a gunman, a bit of a bouncer, but altogether a livewire. He stands over and behind his chief and manipulates the neck muscles.* SARA, *still wearing the frock of the previous scene, sits quietly in her big chair.* RUDI *stands beside her. A cry of pain from* CLEVENGER.]

OCKLEFORD.   Now, it's all right, Chief. It's all right.

CLEVENGER.   No, it isn't all right! A still neck's a damn painful thing!

OCKLEFORD.   As Socrates said: Pleasure's so close to pain, if you go after one you're likely to get the other.

CLEVENGER.   Where did you get that, Ockleford?

OCKLEFORD.   Off some headache tablets an acquaintance of mine takes for sluggish liver.

CLEVENGER.   Might make a good text for a Sunday page.

OCKLEFORD. Sounds pretty cynical to me for Sunday.

CLEVENGER. You may be right. Go on with your report.

OCKLEFORD. There's no more news of the *Farragut* sinking yet. I got through to the White House but the President's resting. They didn't want to disturb him. I wasn't sure you'd like being disturbed in here.

> [SARA's *glance appeals for* RUDI's *sympathy.* RUDI *gives no sign.*]

He's up in the air and will be till you get there. I told 'em we're doing our best, only this isn't what's known as flying weather. Ceiling zero, visibility zero all the way to the Lakes. Ready, Chief?

CLEVENGER. Ready.

> [OCKLEFORD *bends for the grip on Clevenger's neck which is the climax of all osteopathic treatment.*]

OCKLEFORD. You're resisting me.

CLEVENGER. How can I help resisting when I know . . .

> [*The jerk and the neck is cracked.* CLEVENGER, *released, sits up and moves his head carefully.*]

That feels better. Always been susceptible to stiff necks.

> [*Then, sentimentally*]:

You remember, Sara?

SARA. I'm afraid you concealed that side of your nature from me.

CLEVENGER. Yes, of course. I would have. A young man's vanity in physical fitness. Ah, well . . .

> [*He rises.* OCKLEFORD *hands him his collar.*]

Unusual combination of talents Ockleford's got. First rate secretary. Downright genius at massage. Began his career with the six-day bicycle races. Came to me first as a body-guard. Like two-in-one combinations. Makes fewer around me. The fewer the trustier.

> [*To* OCKLEFORD]:

Tie.

> [OCKLEFORD *delivers*. CLEVENGER *proceeds to put himself in order.*]

We'll lay over tonight. And I'll accept your invitation to put me up, Sara. I didn't like that hotel. They don't keep their steam heat under control.

> [*To* RUDI]:

Send down for my bags, Garrison.

> [RUDI *starts to go, but* SARA's *hand stops him.*]

Vest.

> [OCKLEFORD *delivers.*]

Might be a bang-up feature in steam heat and how it's soft-ening our national stamina. Call Curry in New York to-morrow morning. I want figures in Washington on what our American Radiator advertising's worth to us. Start calling at nine and tell me what time you reach him.

> [*To* SARA]:

Always try to keep track of when my executives get to their offices.

> [*To* OCKLEFORD]:

Coat.

> [OCKLEFORD *delivers.*]

And I wish you'd get through to our boys in Rome and Paris. I want the real low-down on this Farragut business.

[*He stands frowning a moment, then, to* RUDI]:

What is it they call you? Rudi?

RUDI. That's right, Mr. Clevenger.

CLEVENGER. If your name's Robert, why don't they call you Bob?

RUDI. I couldn't say.

CLEVENGER. Was your name ever Rudolph?

RUDI. Never.

CLEVENGER. Damn peculiar.

[*Then to* OCKLEFORD]:

That's all, Ockleford.

[*Then to* RUDI, *as* OCKLEFORD *goes into the hall, closing the door after him*]:

That's all for you, too. I came here to renew old times with your sister-in-law. Don't you think her connections by marriage might give me a chance?

[SARA'S *hand is again out to stop* RUDI'S *departure, but* RUDI *goes none the less and in a rage, closing the door after him.* CLEVENGER *continues meanwhile and regardless, to* SARA]:

Only fair to tell you I didn't enjoy my lunch. Who was that young fellow who wouldn't speak to me?

SARA. [*Self-controlled*]: Martin Holme is the son of a dispossessed farmer and the grandson of a pioneer friend of Rudi's father and I brought him up as an elder brother to Roger. Now he's going to marry my daughter Joan and I'm pleased about that because he's a very fine and very brilliant young man. With good reason for feeling coldly towards you.

CLEVENGER.   Don't tell me about it. I only wanted to get the family straight. I've got the Booth Tarkington background: the fine old American house . . .

[SARA *feels the hurt of that.*]

. . . more than adequate income from a nice little family business. Call no man master, no, nor partner, even!

[SARA *is on her feet.*]

Did I hear you speak of entertaining tonight?

SARA.   Haven't you heard about Christmas dinner on Christmas?

CLEVENGER.   I suppose it's too late to call that off?

SARA.   I don't want to call it off!

CLEVENGER.   I only meant that it seems a pity to interrupt this reunion of ours with a lot of outsiders.

SARA.   They're not outsiders to me! You can have your dinner alone in here if you want! Why did I let you into the house this morning?

CLEVENGER.   To see what I'd be like after all these years.

SARA.   You haven't changed much. You come hurtling across the continent in a plane and drop down out of a blizzard and for what? You've done nothing since you came here but jump from bright object to bright object like a baboon!

CLEVENGER.   That's my vitality that I'm famous for.

SARA.   Vitality certainly is God's gift to lightweights!

CLEVENGER.   Me?

SARA.   I don't suppose any one's ever called you a lightweight before! I was thinking of you, though, a few years ago in Milan in Italy. They were having a public dance competition and we went to pass the evening watching it, and the prize was won by a dapper, elderly Austrian nobleman. Winning dance prizes was his life's passion, he told us. His name was Von Berchtold. Do you remember his name?

CLEVENGER. He was the Austrian prime minister who wrote the utimatum to Serbia and started that other war in 1914.

SARA. It's when one sees the leaders of millions like Von Berchtold and you that one's heart grows heavy for trusting humanity, Jim. I wish you'd go on to Washington and leave me in peace.

[*Blandly he takes her arm and seats her on the sofa beside him.*]

CLEVENGER. It's exactly what I knew it would be to see you again. Like Napoleon coming back to Josephine.

SARA. I shouldn't be good in the part. Need I say more?

CLEVENGER. You were in love with me once!

SARA. Don't I remember?

CLEVENGER. Well, I thought you would, but I didn't expect you to say so.

SARA. That's the past. I'm involved in the present now.

CLEVENGER. You don't fit in, Sara! This isn't for you!

SARA. You know I just might be the best judge of that.

CLEVENGER. It's not for you, Sara! It's not for you!

SARA. I've had both public triumphs and private peace. Enough of both to know which I like best.

CLEVENGER. I can't believe you! I don't want to believe you.

SARA.   You've waited twenty years for your chance to patronize me and I shan't be petty enough to spoil your fun. Only you forget I was put on the stage before I was six and got my picture of life from the plays we played then. They were nice plays and about nice people who lived in big houses in peace and security.

[*This hurts again, but* CLEVENGER *does not notice.*]

CLEVENGER.   Is that any excuse for living out here in the sticks?

SARA.   You call it the sticks. I call it America.

CLEVENGER.   That has the sound of civic-mindedness!

SARA.   You should know I'm too lazy to be civic-minded. Except the symphony. I *do* work on that. I fall innocently in love with all the conductors and make them engage Rachmaninoff every season.

CLEVENGER.   I remember your weakness for music.

SARA.   You never shared it.

CLEVENGER.   Oh, I don't know!

[*He clears his throat and performs*]:

> "And when I tell them
>   How wonderful you are,
>   They'll never believe me!
>   They'll never believe me!"

[*Then*]:

You remember Julia Sanderson?

SARA.   With the utmost affection and pleasure. For herself, though. Not because you paid for the tickets.

[*He is dashed.*]

CLEVENGER.   What have you done with your great gifts, Sara?

SARA. I've lived the life I wanted to live and liked it, and learned quite a few things you wouldn't know are important. How pleasant an evening alone can be, for example, with a long book and a great deal of coffee. That it's a great mistake to carry a watch, because no time matters except time to one's self. I've been singularly and completely contented here.

[*Again the room and her troubles overcome her.*]

CLEVENGER. Do you never regret what you gave up for this?

SARA. If I read that melting eye correctly, I do not regret you.

CLEVENGER. Why didn't you marry me, Sara?

SARA. Jim, how boring! You haven't thought of me for . . .

CLEVENGER. Now I've seen you again . . . You're the only thing I've ever wanted that I couldn't get.

SARA. That's fairly cheap of you.

CLEVENGER. We *were* in love. Why didn't you marry me?

SARA. Well, if you must go digging into the past, you never asked me to marry you!

[CLEVENGER *is shocked.*]

CLEVENGER. You can't be right about that!

SARA. I am, though. The idea was to add my latchkey to quite a collection. I had my own waiting line at the box office then. I couldn't see myself standing in yours after the show.

CLEVENGER. But I did ask you, Sara! I remember!

SARA. The night I told you I was marrying Paul. I didn't count that. The gong had already gone.

CLEVENGER.   You never cared for your husband as you
did for me.

SARA.   [*Honest indignation*]: That isn't true!

CLEVENGER.   You only married to get away from me.

SARA.   Oh, that's really annoying!

CLEVENGER.   You didn't marry again after he died.

SARA.   And what does that prove?

CLEVENGER.   Don't the happily married always try it
again?

SARA.   All this wit and wisdom! I should hate you to
think, though, that I haven't had chances. Now, isn't it
about time for another osteopathic interlude?

CLEVENGER.   You should have married me, Sara. I
should have given you all this and more.

[*She turns furiously on him.*]

SARA.   You couldn't have given me any of it! Nor understood why I wanted its peace and permanence! And
if you've turned up here today for no better reason than
an impulse to sort through old valentines, I'm sorry, Jim,
but I'm just not in the mood!

CLEVENGER.   I'm not here to sort old valentines. I'm
here because, once I'd got safely down out of this storm,
I thought of the curious gift you used to have for setting
me straight in almost any dilemma. You're still the strong-
est and clearest person I've ever known.

SARA.   And what am I expected to say to that? That
I'm afraid I've become just a mousy widow lady? I
haven't! Go on to Washington! We've all got dilemmas of
our own these days!

CLEVENGER.   You and I share the same dilemma,
Sara.

SARA.   I doubt that somehow.

CLEVENGER.   As people of property we're both pre-occupied with self-preservation.

> [*This startles her. For a moment she thinks he may know about her predicament. Then she recovers herself.*]

SARA.   But not in the same sense. I've been through that once today and solved it, what's more, so . . .

> [JOAN *enters from the hall, leaving the door open.*]

JOAN.   Mother . . .

CLEVENGER.   We're very busy in here!

JOAN.   But Mr. Clevenger's pilot's come.

> [STEVE ANDREWS *enters, with an appreciative glance at Joan as he passes her. In his late twenties, he is handsome, romantic, thoroughly sure of himself and quietly flashy about it.*]

STEVE.   How do you do?

> [SARA *would greet him, but* CLEVENGER *interferes*]

CLEVENGER.   What are you doing here?

STEVE.   I didn't like that hotel any better than you did. You had a dreamy kind of look when you left there this morning. If you can improve your conditions, why can't I? So when that chauffeur came for the bags just now . . .

CLEVENGER.   Whose bags did you give him?

STEVE.   Yours and mine both, Chief. All there were to give.

CLEVENGER. But you can't plant yourself on Mrs. Garrison!

STEVE. Why not? They told me down there it's a great big, comfortable house. And it is. And I'm always welcome wherever I go.

> [*His smile is the more charming for his impudence.*]

It's peaceful out here, too. Any idea what goes on downtown?

JOAN. What?

STEVE. There are those who'd call it a riot. Maybe they're only celebrating not having any work to do these days. I've been known to celebrate a bit of leisure myself. Not quite that way, though. There I am in the hotel dining room, sitting quietly over my tea, when a brick comes crashing through the plate glass window and knocks the old-fashioned right out of my hand.

CLEVENGER. Things weren't so bad downtown that you had to . . .

STEVE. Oh, no! I just brought them up as an excuse for joining you in the comforts of home.

SARA. You're welcome here, Mr. Andrews. I read every word that's printed about you famous flyers. Your father must be very proud of you.

STEVE. My father's dead.

> [SARA *is surprised to hear it.*]

CLEVENGER. Of course I'm proud of him.

> [STEVE *is surprised.*]

It's all right. She knew all about your mother and me.

STEVE. There's a young girl in the room. I don't think it's right to talk about things like illegitimacy with a young girl in the room.

[*To* SARA]:

Might as well call me "Steve," though. Every one does.

SARA. That's the hallmark of great, great greatness, these days, isn't it? To be "Steve" to the public. Will you tell me a lot about flying in China and what Lhassa looks like? I've always had a weakness for mysterious, far-away cities. Without any ambition to see them for myself.

STEVE. Shall I tell you now or later?

> [*But* ROGER *appears excitedly from the hall—
> ski knickers and galoshes plastered with snow
> —accompanied by* PATIENCE *and* MICHAEL, *both
> in tears.*]

ROGER. Have you seen what's going on in the street?
SARA. No. What?
ROGER. Shut up, you kids! You're all right now.

> [*The* CHILDREN *clutch one another and subside
> somewhat as* ROGER *comes into the room.*]

I was dragging the kids in their sled and all of a sudden there they were, all around us . . .

JOAN. Who?
ROGER. The unemployed by the look of 'em! They must be the unemployed! And out here in this part of town, too! Can you beat it?

> [*He has gone to the window. The others are follow-
> ing.*]

STEVE.   I'd keep back from those windows, Mrs. Garrison. Those are the boys who just got my old-fashioned.

[DORIS *enters from the parlor, followed by* JOHN.]

DORIS.   Where are the children?

JOHN.   Are they all right?

DORIS.   They're terribly frightened!

JOAN.   Listen! You can't hear a sound!

STEVE.   That's the snow underfoot.

JOAN.   The snow doesn't seem so peaceful now.

STEVE.   You'd think they'd be singing or carrying placards.

JOAN.   There's one with a placard. I can't read what it says.

DORIS.   [*From the hall*]:   They shouldn't be permitted in this part of town!

JOHN.   Oh, I don't know! Not a bad idea for 'em to show themselves out here, to the people who've got the money.

[DORIS *flashes an angry glance at him as she starts the* CHILDREN *up the stair.* RUDI *and* MARTIN *enter from the parlor.*]

RUDI.   I'm on my way down to *The Globe*, Sara. Don't want to miss too much, even on Christmas.

[*He has got his hat and coat from the hall table.*] Back in time for dinner.

[*He goes towards the front door.*]

JOAN.   They're not even asking for food. Just marching by. Can't we do something, Mother?

[SARA *turns as though to ask what.* JOHN *has come back into the room.*]

At least give them what food we've got in the house.

STEVE.   What would we eat for dinner?

MARTIN.   That's not the way, Joan.

STEVE.   I'd organize those boys into an army and rent it out. Mercenaries, you know. Keep 'em out of trouble.

[JOHN *eyes him darkly.*]

I suppose there'd be feeling against it.

MARTIN.   I should think there might be.

STEVE.   There always is against anything practical.

JOAN.   There weren't many of them. That's the end.

[DORIS *has paused on the stair, the* CHILDREN *going on up and out of sight.*]

DORIS.   There may be more! Pull down the window shades, Sara.

JOHN.   That's not the way either.

SARA.   We can't shut it out. We could board up the windows and seal over the doors, but the world's sickness would seep down the chimney like fog and up through the floor like smoke.

CLEVENGER.   You're right, Sara. It would.

[*Then suddenly, and very loud*]:

Ockleford!

[*Sensation. Silence.* OCKLEFORD *enters.*]

Where in hell's the news I wanted on that ship?

OCKLEFORD.   The story in Rome as confirmed by the two survivors of the *Farragut's* crew is as follows: At noon yesterday she was stopped by a French submarine. The French must have known she was carrying contraband to the Italians. An Italian plane comes out of the clouds,

so the French let go a torpedo without waiting to search.
The *Farragut* broke all records on her way to the bottom.
Two survivors were all the load the Italian plane could
carry.

CLEVENGER.   Two saved and how many lost?

OCKLEFORD.   Seventeen.

JOAN.   How awful! How perfectly
awful!

JOHN.   We just have to remember
not to let ourselves . . .   [*Almost
                                                  simultaneous*]
DORIS.   It doesn't seem like I
could stand to hear any more . . .

STEVE.   Seventeen! Say, we
stepped into it that time!

CLEVENGER.   Quiet, for God's sake! ! !

> [*Quiet is restored.* SARA *looks at him, amazed. He
> catches her eye, then*]:

I couldn't hear myself think.

> [*The company is not unnaturally offended.* DORIS
> *goes on up the stair and out of sight.*]

That's all for now, Ockleford. I'll call you when I want
anything else.

> [*He moves away, smoking nervously.* OCKLEFORD
> *goes.*]

SARA.   [*Low*]: Joan, don't you want to take Mr. Andrews up and find him a place to sleep? There are all those
bags, too. Roger will lend a hand.

> [ROGER *is in fact just starting up the stair. He
> pauses, hearing his name.* JOAN *turns back into
> the hall with* STEVE.]

JOAN. [*To* STEVE]: This is my brother Roger. Mr. Andrews is Mr. Clevenger's pilot.

[ROGER *comes down to shake hands.*]

ROGER. Andrews? Not *Steve* Andrews?
STEVE. I'm afraid so.

[ROGER *is overwhelmed.*]

ROGER. Well, for God's sake!

[*Then, as* STEVE *has picked up two aeroplane suitcases*]:

Here, give me those!

[*He takes one of the bags, leading the way up the stair, chattering back over his shoulder.*]

You're the best Christmas present I've had this year! How many more great men does Mother know?

[*In the meanwhile, however,* SARA *has signed to* JOHN *to leave and he goes now, closing the door after him, shutting the young people out and leaving* SARA *with her eye fixed hard on* CLEVENGER.]

CLEVENGER. Thank you.

[*He resumes his restless movement about the room.* SARA *draws a deep breath. Then*]:

SARA. Why is the sinking of this ship of such extreme interest to you at this moment?

CLEVENGER. [*Evasive*]: I'm a newspaper publisher. This is news. She was flying the American flag and named for an American naval hero and the French sank her the day before Christmas and seventeen young American sailors went down with her.

SARA.   Everything but the ship and the sailors is sentiment. The ship had no business in the war trade, had she? And the sailors must have known she had none.

CLEVENGER.   If we can take this, we can take anything.

SARA.   We can take it, can't we?

CLEVENGER.   I don't know.

[*She is alarmed but can still think craftily.*]

SARA.   I can't help suspecting that you want an excuse for leading us into worse trouble, Jim.

[*His eyes narrow a little before he answers her.*]

CLEVENGER.   Leading's one thing I've never attempted, Sara. I've built up my power by following. I was born with a gift for guessing what my readers want and with too much shrewdness to offer them anything else.

[*But he concludes murkily.*]

Now my power and I have been summoned to Washington. And I don't know what my readers want of me now.

SARA.   [*Very clear*]: They don't want to fight.

CLEVENGER.   They want only the right that we've taken from them—and don't call me a cynic for quoting Jefferson—to "fatten on the follies of the Old World."

[*Then, violently*]:

We can't stand much more of this neutrality, Sara! Sooner or later, sooner or later, some one . . .

[*His dilemma again moves him restlessly about the room.*]

SARA.   [*Increasing alarm*]: Some one, Jim?

CLEVENGER.   [*Almost to himself*]: Nor would it take much. . . . It would take very little . . .

[SARA, *though steady, is watching him sharply.*]

SARA.   To push us into this war?

[*He is startled.*]

CLEVENGER.   I didn't say that! I didn't say anything!

SARA.   [*Now thoroughly alarmed*]: What are you going to do in Washington, Jim?

CLEVENGER.   God in his wisdom may know—I wish I did! If you think they make any more sense in Washington than your idealistic brothers-in-law make here! The same confusion, here, there and everywhere! The same halfway, half-baked, half-assed thinking!

[*He recovers himself.*]

I beg your pardon. I forgot myself.

[*But his fury bursts out again.*]

By God, though, I mean to prevent the President's using me and my power any further until I've determined a few things for myself!

SARA.   You don't want us at war, do you?

[CLEVENGER *moves quickly to his own defence.*]

CLEVENGER.   No man hates war more than I do, Sara! Eighteen months ago, when your pacifist friends were passing resolutions on the horrors of war, I was making my plans for the horrors of peace. I knew their neutrality didn't stand a chance, with the depression it was sure to bring on us, if the country were told half of what would be going on. So I built up a dike around the country. Not only in my own papers but in every paper where I could make my influence felt. My fellow publishers loathe me but listen to me, because they know I'm a great newspaperman! And the President's grateful to my dike and me for the news and propaganda we've kept out of print. So it's my work that we've no war party here!

[*But the pride of his tone falters.*]

That was all in the beginning, though. When there was no doubt what the readers wanted.

SARA. There should be no doubt now of what they want.

CLEVENGER. There may be some of what's best for them.

[*And he breaks out*]:

Those men out there! They're the price of this neutrality on parade!

[*Then he pulls himself up.*]

I don't know. I don't . . .

[*Once again the deep breath she needs to steady herself. Then*]:

SARA. Do you know the look of the landscape just at twilight? When all the colors are clear and easy to see and the distance is sharp to the horizon? If we could hold that moment I think we should go wrong very seldom.

[*She goes to him passionately.*]

I'm sorry for the easy, cheap things I've said today! If I have, as you say, some gift to make you see clearly—I don't know what it can be, but make use of me now! Not just as the woman you once loved, who once loved you! There are millions like me who find life too good for violence! Oh, dear, it all sounds so trite! It's been said so often!

[*Her hands are reached out to him. Genuinely moved, he takes them in his own.*]

CLEVENGER.   I'm not making love to you, Sara, when I tell you that my only impulse is to let Washington wait and sit here in this house until looking at you makes my course clear to me. Will you give me guidance and an omen?

[*She shakes her head, worried, yet smiling at him.*]

SARA.   If you'll heed any guidance or omen you get from me, Jim . . .

CLEVENGER.   I promise to.

[*She smiles. Then*]:

SARA.   You know, Jim, there's something appealing about you, after all.

[*He looks up quickly. The curtain falls.*]

THE THIRD SCENE

[*The curtain rises again almost immediately.*]

The lamps are lighted but the curtains are not drawn across the windows and the snow out of doors falls through the blue of a northern twilight.

[CLEVENGER *is seated in* SARA's *big chair asleep, a handkerchief over his head.* JOAN *stands over him, watching him gravely.* MARTIN *stands in the parlor door. A pause.* CLEVENGER *stirs.* JOAN *glances towards* MARTIN *to make sure that he is still there.* CLEVENGER *awakens, removes the handkerchief from his face, sees* JOAN *and is not pleased.*]

JOAN.   I thought I'd make myself felt if I stared long enough.

CLEVENGER.   [*With great dignity*]: Whenever I have something peculiarly difficult to think out I sleep to give my subconscious a chance.

JOAN.   Now's your chance, Martin. You'll be sorry your whole life if you don't take it.

[CLEVENGER *turns as* MARTIN *comes forward.* CLEVENGER *is surprised,* MARTIN *embarrassed, but* JOAN *continues with complete steadiness.*]

Martin thinks it isn't good manners to bring up his grudge while you're under our roof. But you're not staying under our roof more than a few hours longer and Martin's grudge is every bit as important as the fact that you once gave Mother an ermine coat.

[CLEVENGER *looks from one to the other in bewilderment. Then, to* MARTIN]:

CLEVENGER. So you've got a grudge, have you?

MARTIN. Only for having me fired from my job.

[CLEVENGER *shakes his head.*]

CLEVENGER. I never heard of you till this morning, Mr. Holme.

JOAN. Doctor Holme.

CLEVENGER. Then I'm sure you're wrong, because I don't employ doctors.

MARTIN. I'm an economist, not a physician. And I was teaching in the University of Los Angeles till your paper there forced me out as a Communist.

CLEVENGER. Oho!

JOAN. You do remember him now?

CLEVENGER. No. But I begin to see what he's driving at.

[*But* MARTIN *makes himself clear with undismayed good humor.*]

MARTIN. I don't want you to think I minded about the job. Teaching economics is really a kind of racket. Unless one's prepared each year to retract half the gospel one handed out the year before. And that only adds to the general confusion.

CLEVENGER. Your scientific attitude does you great credit, Doctor. You can't be a very orothodox Communist.

JOAN. But he's no Communist at all!

MARTIN. I wish I were. It would make both living and thinking a whole lot simpler.

CLEVENGER.   Well, after all, Communism's only a kind of trade name for all kinds of thinking one doesn't happen to relish. Unless of course one happens to *be* a Communist. In which case the term Fascism may be employed for the same purpose and with the same poetic disregard for making sense.

MARTIN.   But we teachers consider ourselves rather special people, Mr. Clevenger—chock full of the free, inquiring, critical spirit. And specially privileged, no matter whose corns we tread on.

CLEVENGER.   This doesn't mean you've been attacking me?

JOAN.   You know he has!

CLEVENGER.   I'm more than embarrassed, but this is the first I've heard about that, too.

   [*Then, back to* MARTIN]:

Why don't you tell me what you want of me?

MARTIN.   Well, I don't know.

JOAN.   He wants satisfaction!

CLEVENGER.   What kind? An apology? It's made. A published retraction? I'll arrange it tomorrow. I'll call Ockleford.

   [*He is on his way and moving towards the door.*]

I'll give you a job.

MARTIN.   Oh, no! No, thank you!

CLEVENGER.   [*The best of good humor*]: Men of your type often like me to make the offer so they can have the satisfaction of turning it down.

JOAN.   It's emotional satisfaction that he wants!

CLEVENGER.   Won't he get more of that from you than he would from me?

MARTIN. I could wish you hadn't come here, Mr. Clevenger. And the same for your famous aviating son. Neither materialist nor hero is good for us here.

CLEVENGER. I never thought to hear an educator say that! Don't you know that every fresh contact opens a new mental door on life? You've still a great deal to learn. You think you're a victim of my political bigotry. Or of some desire on my part to get even with you. You're no such thing. Your quarrel's with legitimate business enterprise. My Los Angeles paper has been losing circulation. At an alarming rate for such an inferior paper. My readers out there are acutely interested in a thing called Americanism. That's a kind of trade name they use for everything their taxes go to support. Up to the point where the taxes become a burden.

[*He ventures to buttonhole* MARTIN.]

And a Red raid, particularly on a University faculty, can be made to provide all the gladiatorial action the modern taxpayer seems to require before he'll read the paper I want him to read. And the worst that can possibly be said against me is that I interpret our civil liberties in the classic American way: that is, to my own private advantage as a conservative member of a conservative society. And the difference between me and the rest of my kind is that they're afraid to admit what they are and I'm not. Now, if I've explained myself with sufficient candor, I'll go dress for dinner and leave Steve the task of completing our joint educational program.

[*And he goes up the stair. But* JOAN *leaps into the breach.*]

JOAN.   You stood up to him! I don't think he's used to men standing up to him!

MARTIN.   Am I still on my feet?

JOAN.   You're ten thousand times the man he is!

MARTIN.   He doesn't know that.

JOAN.   Why did Mother ever let that pair into the house? Such people spread poison wherever they go!

MARTIN.   He's right, though, about my having a lot to learn. And I thank him for teaching me quite a bit of it.

JOAN.   Martin!

MARTIN.   He's shown me that our kind can't stand in the middle of the road much longer. Sooner or later we'll have to choose one of the sidewalks.

JOAN.   We're young! We'll make out all right!

MARTIN.   Where? With those men marching by just now?

JOAN.   We don't belong with them!

MARTIN.   With Clevenger then?

JOAN.   Oh, no!

[*Then*]:

Martin! I'm frightened, Martin! Let's go away! Some place where we'll be safe from everything that pair stands for! And from everything else!

MARTIN.   Run away, Joan? Shame on you!

JOAN.   Far away! Let's get married next week and go to . . . to Fairbanks, Alaska!

[*Now* MARTIN *is laughing.*]

MARTIN.   What would we do in Fairbanks?

JOAN.   [*Who can't imagine*]: We . . . we could plant trees there! They must need trees in Fairbanks! I see

Fairbanks without any trees! And that would give you something to do with your hands while you're thinking things out and . . .

[*But his arms are around her.*]

MARTIN. Oh, Joan! My darling Joan!

[ROGER *enters from the pantry with cocktail glasses on a tray.*]

ROGER. How about a drink to get dressed on, lovers?

MARTIN. Why not? Drink deadens the mind and makes trouble less troublesome.

ROGER. So Steve says.

JOAN. [*Surprised and not pleased*]: Steve!

[STEVE *enters, also from the pantry, and shaking a very large cocktail shaker.*]

ROGER. I've turned the bar over to Steve for the evening. This is his arrangement of rum, vermouth and cointreau. It's called a "Steve Andrews," isn't it, Steve?

STEVE. Only by the select public I make it for. Martinis still hold their own with the mob.

ROGER. It has to be made in Steve's own shaker, too. Look, Martin! He's carried it with him every place he's flown and every time he shakes 'em up for a party he has the place and date engraved on the side!

MARTIN. That will come in handy when you write your autobiography.

STEVE. Got the idea from an old war flyer. A fellow from Pittsburgh.

ROGER. My father was a war flyer. Did I tell you that?

STEVE. That's what planes were meant for. War. The

rest of it's just endurance and navigation. War's real flying.

ROGER.   Steve's got me all hopped up about flying. Doesn't see why I wouldn't make a swell flyer. Says any man with my nerve for winter sports . . .

STEVE.   Sure. Why not?

[JOAN *finds herself disconcerted by the direct admiration with which* STEVE *persists in regarding her.* MARTIN *has been examining the shaker.*]

MARTIN.   Look, Joan! Here's your old stamping ground. Cairo. Luxor. Khartoum.

STEVE.   What? Oh, yes! Egypt.

JOAN.   [*To* MARTIN]: Some day, Martin, when the world's all straight again and licking its wounds, you'll take me back to Luxor and we'll ride horses out over a pale brass morning desert and sail up and down the Nile under the moon and drink marvellous gin fizzes at the Winter Palace and say how much better the social system is now than it was when Pharaoh rode in his barge to the temples at Karnak.

[*But* STEVE *lounges towards them.*]

STEVE.   Think so?

MARTIN.   Don't you?

STEVE.   You write books, don't you?

MATIN.   I? Well, I've written a couple.

[STEVE *seats himself comfortably on the sofa.*]

STEVE.   I like seeing things for myself better than reading about 'em. What are your books about?

MARTIN.   Well, about the changing social system.

STEVE.   Well, knocking around, I've picked up a few

ideas on that. Egypt, now. That was a trip I took for the papers. To look for the Lost Oasis.

ROGER. Bet it isn't lost any more! Bet you found it, Steve!

STEVE. We found a rock pile no one ever noticed before. 'Way out in the Libyan desert. All blighted flint and sand for hundreds of miles. No water at all, so there couldn't be any life there. We didn't see so much as a scorpion. But the funny thing was that the rocks were all full of caves. And the walls of the caves were all covered over with drawings. Eight, maybe ten thousand years old. And a lot of the drawings showed the old natives swimming.

JOAN. [*In spite of herself*]: How fascinating! How perfectly . . .

STEVE. What I meant, though, was those prehistorics swimming in a lake that's gone the way of all good geology. Because I can't see that social systems change much. Whether you ride to Karnak in a barge or to Wall Street in a Rolls-Royce, we're still Pharaohs, thank God! It's Nature does the changing in her own good time. From glaciers to Great Lakes. From Lakes to desert.

MARTIN. Oh, it isn't that slow! It really isn't that slow.

STEVE. That's how it looks when you're high enough up to get a load of the works.

ROGER. I can see that! That's how it's looked to me when I've been up!

JOAN. [*To* STEVE]: Didn't I hear Mother saying you'd been to Tibet? To Lhassa?

[*And she sits on the sofa beside him.*]

STEVE.   I went there for the papers, too.

ROGER.   There's more in the shaker. Can I pour?

STEVE.   Sure. Go ahead.

JOAN.   What's it like in Lhassa?

STEVE.   Well, now, I'll tell you. That was a long flight to Lhassa, an awful long flight. And personally *I* was disappointed. It's a filthy town. Cold and bare. No trees.

JOAN.   [*Surprised*]: No trees!

>   [JOHN *appears in the hall—dinner coat—followed by* BUCK ANSON: *short, husky, up from the ranks of skilled labor, forty-five—hat and overcoat.*] .

JOHN.   We can talk in here, Buck. You kids had better be dressing.

MARTIN.   Is it that late already?

JOAN.   Come along, Martin.

>   [*They go out and up the stair.* JOHN *continues to* STEVE *and* ROGER.]

JOHN.   Won't that thing be of more use in the parlor?

>   [SENATOR CALLORY—*tails and white tie—enters from the parlor.*]

See? Your mother's customers are beginning to gather.

>   [*And, as* ROGER *and* STEVE *take the shaker into the parlor*]:

Come in, Buck! Come in! You know Senator Callory, don't you?

BUCK.   I've had the pleasure.

>   [CALLORY *shakes hands, but does not recall the meeting.*]

JOHN. Buck's been our general manager down at the plant—how long is it now, Buck?

BUCK. Well, it's twenty-five years since I first went to work there.

CALLORY. And you've let 'em break in on your Christmas, Mr. Anson?

BUCK. Holidays never was much in my life, Senator. Never took a day off I wasn't glad when it was over.

[RUDI—*also evening dress—has come down the stair and into the room.*]

RUDI. Hello, Buck! Merry Christmas.

BUCK. Guess we'll leave that part out this year, Mr. Garrison.

JOHN. I've already told Buck the worst.

RUDI. Then the rest is soon over.

[*And to* CALLORY]:

Well, Senator, I see you're in on this, too.

CALLORY. Oh, I'm here tonight as a friend of the family . . .

[RUDI's *glance is so sharp that he adds*]:

For Christmas dinner.

RUDI. That's so. Fifty Christmases. And in three weeks—you'll have digested your Christmas dinner by then—you'll go into court, get your receivers appointed and take over. Still as a friend of the family, I suppose?

[CALLORY *does not answer.*]

JOHN. We don't have to take Buck's time up with this.

RUDI. No. Sorry, Buck. No judgment at all. Proceed with the proceedings.

JOHN.   I've got Buck to come over because we'll have to begin laying men off at the plant tomorrow. I couldn't let him wait to hear the bad news with the whole gang in the morning.

RUDI.   [*Horrified*] : Do you mean that when our men go to work tomorrow, the day after Christmas, there won't be any work?

JOHN.   Saturday's payroll already looks pretty big.

CALLORY.   You wouldn't be playing fair with your creditors, Rudi, to let it get any bigger.

RUDI.   You ought to know. Objection withdrawn. Go on.

JOHN.   It's said. That's always the way. You dread these moments and they're over before you know it.

[*To* BUCK] :

Better get your plans for tomorrow lined up tonight. I'll be down early to see you.

BUCK.   Will that be all for now?

JOHN.   I can't think of anything more.

BUCK.   I guess I'll be going then.

RUDI.   Can't we give you a drink?

BUCK.   Any drinking I do tonight I'll do alone. I wish I was ten years younger. Not so easy to find a new job when you're past forty.

RUDI.   At least I'm in the same boat with you.

[*About to pick up his hat and coat,* BUCK *pauses to speak his only protest.*]

BUCK.   We weren't laying off men in the last war. Your father didn't like fighting any better than you, but he was a practical man and he took his profits. And our men'd be better off in the trenches than they'll be in the breadlines.

I'll say this, though. I know you wouldn't have got in so deep if you hadn't been so hell-bent to keep the men working. You'd be better off now if you'd shut down and waited for good times like other firms done. It's tough tittie, that's all.

[*He goes out.* JOHN *follows him.*]

RUDI. [*To* CALLORY]: It's worse than tough tittie! When John told us about this this morning, Sara wanted to go to you and ask you for time. We told her she mustn't. Now I wish I could think of some way to . . .

[CALLORY *will not let him continue.*]

CALLORY. Why say that to me? Garrison Tool and Die's of no use to us! We won't realize fifty cents on the dollar! We're paying the forfeit, not you, if the truth be told! What can I do? My obligation isn't to John or you, or even Sara! It's to our stockholders and depositors!

RUDI. What's become of the old-fashioned family banker? Has he gone the way of the family doctor?

[*But* CALLORY *cuts him off.*]

CALLORY. Let's go to the party!
RUDI. Right. Sorry if I was tactless.

[CLEVENGER *is shouting from above stairs.*]

CLEVENGER. Ockleford!

[*He comes running down the stair—dressed, like the others, for dinner, but in a state of considerable excitement.*]

RUDI. Pipe down about this.

[CALLORY *is surprised.*]

Let Sara keep up her front while he's in the house.

CLEVENGER.   Ockleford! Where are you, Ockleford?

[*He enters the library.*]

The snow's stopped! Have you noticed?

[*He goes to the window to push back the curtain. The snow has, in fact, stopped completely.* CALLORY *signals for* RUDI *to introduce him and draws himself up.*]

RUDI.   Here's the leading citizen of our town, Mr. Clevenger. The Honorable Edward J. Callory, former United States Senator and . . .

CLEVENGER.   [*The briefest handshake*]: Oh, yes!

[*Then to* RUDI]:

Where's that pilot of mine?

[CALLORY, *mortally offended, goes into the parlor. Opening the door, he releases the sound of a company of guests. This happens,—the sound increasing as, presumably, the guests arrive— whenever the parlor door is opened from now on.*]

RUDI.   He should be in drinking a cocktail with the rest.

[OCKLEFORD *enters.*]

CLEVENGER.   Well, get him in here! We can be getting off!

[RUDI *goes into the parlor.* CLEVENGER *turns to* OCKLEFORD.]

Get out in the street. Take a look at the sky. I can't see from indoors.

> [OCKLEFORD *goes out into the hall.* STEVE—*dinner coat—enters from the parlor.*]

STEVE. What's going on?

CLEVENGER. We're going on! Have you looked out the window? The snow's stopped! Get on the phone to the airport! I want up-to-the-minute weather from here to the Lakes.

STEVE. Now? Before dinner?

CLEVENGER. We don't stop for dinner if we can . . .

STEVE. I was making my plans to take off at day-break!

CLEVENGER. *Your* plans!

STEVE. Your old girl's got a damn pretty daughter!

CLEVENGER. [*Angry*]: Didn't I tell you not to get tight tonight?

STEVE. [*Also angry*]: Who's tight?

CLEVENGER. You've been drinking cocktails?

STEVE. What's that got to do with getting tight?

CLEVENGER. Stand on your hands!

STEVE. Why should I stand on my hands?

CLEVENGER. If you can't stand on your hands you're not sober enough to take me up in the air!

> [*With the ease of the accomplished gymnast* STEVE *is already standing on his hands. But* SARA, *most beautifully dressed for the evening, is coming down the stair.*]

STEVE. Does that satisfy you?

CLEVENGER. Does that what?

STEVE.   I can't talk! My mouth's full of spit!

SARA.   I should think it might be.

[STEVE *returns to normalcy.*]

Are you all right?

STEVE.   I was just demonstrating how all right I am!

SARA.   I'm told that's the only way to look at a sunset.

[*She turns to* CLEVENGER.]

I'm sorry to hear you're leaving. But I couldn't help hearing. Well, my poor little dinner started off without lions. It can go back now to its former simplicity.

[OCKLEFORD *returns.*]

OCKLEFORD.   Can't see the sky on account of the street lights, Chief. Feels steadier, though, and colder.

[*But* CLEVENGER, *his eye fastened on* SARA, *waves him back.*]

CLEVENGER.   [*To* STEVE]: Never mind the air port. We'll stay over after all.

STEVE.   Then I can go back to my vital interests.

[*He returns to the parlor.* OCKLEFORD *retires to the hall.*]

CLEVENGER.   You're looking more than usually beautiful, Sara.

[SARA *smooths her dress.*]

SARA.   I did my best for you. I'm glad you noticed.

CLEVENGER.   Let's sit right down again and go on talking about the good old days.

SARA.   Jim! All those people in there!

CLEVENGER.   Oh, hang those people!

SARA. We covered the good old days this afternoon.

CLEVENGER. Yet they seem as real as ever to me to-night. Why don't you feel more sentiment about them?

SARA. One can leave things in the ice box just so long.

CLEVENGER. You win! I can't stand ridicule!

[*She softens.*]

SARA. Have I hurt your feelings? Shall I show you something?

CLEVENGER. What?

[*She goes to a drawer in the desk for a photograph which she brings to him.*]

SARA. It's what's known as a faded old photograph. I found it in my theatre trunk in the attic. That's a very affectionate inscription, Jim. I hope you meant it.

CLEVENGER. [*Of the photograph*]: That's a strong chin, Sara.

SARA. [*She is looking at him*]: Which?

[*Then, back to the photograph*]:

Oh, that one!

CLEVENGER. The years have been kinder to you than they have to me.

SARA. You were a very attractive young man, Jim. I told you you haven't changed.

CLEVENGER. You weren't being very complimentary when you said that.

SARA. And I might so easily have been! It's rather nice, I find, to be with a man who isn't suffering from ideological jitters.

CLEVENGER. In this house, that must seem very restful.

SARA.   It does.

[ROGER *appears in the hall to call up the stair.*]

ROGER.   Mother! Where are you, Mother?

[SARA *turns, startled out of her moment of sentiment.*]

Every one's waiting! What terrible manners, Mother!
SARA.   [*Too much on her dignity*]: Really, Rog! I
don't need you to remind me of my manners!

[*Then, tossing the photograph into the desk, she
turns back to* CLEVENGER.]

Are you ready to make your entrance?

[*He takes her arm. They move together towards
the parlor.* ROGER *goes ahead to open the door.*
VOICES *greet them.*]

VOICES.   Merry Christmas, Sara! . . .
Sara, where have you been? . . .
Don't you know you're having a party here
tonight? . . .
Sara, how lovely you look! . . .
Merry Christmas, Sara! . . .

[STEVE'S *cocktail shaker is loud as the curtain
falls.*]

THE FOURTH SCENE

[*The curtain rises almost immediately.*]

It is the day after Christmas. The tree as before, but no fire now and out of doors the shine of a brilliant, bitter morning.

> [JOHN, *back in civilian clothes again, is pacing to and fro across the room.* DORIS—*hat and fur coat—sits nervously on the edge of a chair. From the street beyond the parlor windows comes the diminishing clamor of* SHOUTS *and* CAT-CALLS, *through which the bell of a* POLICE PATROL *fades into the distance. Then* MARY *enters, followed by a* POLICE SERGEANT.]

JOHN.   Well, officer, what was it this time?

THE SERGEANT.   Had to run another one of 'em in, Mr. Garrison.

JOHN.   What had this one done that you ran him in for it?

THE SERGEANT.   He come out with a placard that you wouldn't of cared for.

JOHN.   What did the placard say?

[*The* SERGEANT *hesitates.*]

Did you see it, Mary?

[ROGER *appears in the parlor door.*]

MARY.   It said: "Step out of your fine warm house into the cold with our children and us."

THE SERGEANT.   It was rougher than that.

JOHN.   Those men out there are the old employes of our company, officer, who've lost their jobs through no fault of their own. And if it gives them the least satisfaction to picket this house they are not to be interfered with!

[MARTIN *appears in the parlor door.*]

THE SERGEANT.   You're making things pretty tough for us, Mr. Garrison. This picketing private homes in the residence district ain't a precedent we can afford to encourage!

JOHN.   We pay the taxes on this property. When we want police protection we'll ask for it.

THE SERGEANT.   O.K., Mr. Garrison.

[JOAN *has come tumbling down the stair.*]

JOAN.   What is going on outside, Uncle John?

JOHN.   It's nothing to get any one excited! We've had to lay off a few men down at the plant. For business reasons.

[RUDI *enters from the parlor.*]

And they quite naturally resent being laid off and they've every right to show their resentment.

> [*The* SERGEANT, *having gone into the hall and disappeared towards the front door with* MARY, *is now, as presumably he appears in the street, greeted by a fresh outburst of* CAT-CALLS.]

RUDI.   And I hope they can stick it long enough to . . .

ROGER.   To what? Watch us walk out of our fine warm house forever?

MARTIN.   That might give them some satisfiaction.

JOAN. [*Frantic*]: What are you all talking about?

JOHN. [*His nerve breaking*]: Take her some place out of here and tell her!

MARTIN. Come into the dining room, Joan, and get your breakfast.

> [*They go out into the hall and turn past the pantry.*]

DORIS. You're beyond me! All of you just beyond me!

> [*She is on her feet, shaking.*]

I'm going home to the country and get my children where they'll be safe!

> [*And she makes for the stair. But MARY has returned from the front door, followed by the SERGEANT and two other POLICE OFFICERS. The sight of them is a red rag to JOHN.*]

JOHN. What do you cops want now?

> [*Before the POLICE can answer, CLEVENGER has entered from the hall.*]

CLEVENGER. They've come in at my invitation, Mr. Garrison. It's cold guarding a house on a morning like this. I've suggested that Sara's cook serve the officers coffee.

JOHN. Aren't you taking a good deal on yourself?

> [CLEVENGER, *ignoring him, has gone to the* POLICE.]

CLEVENGER. I asked for the Sergeant in command outside.

> [*The* SERGEANT *steps forward.*]

THE SERGEANT.   That's me, sir.

CLEVENGER.   I'm J. M. Clevenger. In case you don't know my name, I own *The Morning Eagle*.

[*But the* SERGEANT *has already touched his cap.*]

How many men have you got on duty here?

THE SERGEANT.   Six including me, sir.

CLEVENGER.   I want that force doubled and kept on night and day.

RUDI.   Damn it, Mr. Clevenger, you must have heard my brother!

CLEVENGER.   I haven't the slightest objection to your wet-nursing those pickets, but I reserve the right to feel uneasy for your sister-in-law. And in view of the fact that my paper owns the police force in this town . . .

[*He is waving the police out. But* JOHN *has his
counter proposal ready.*]

JOHN.   Mary, ask Anna to make a lot of coffee, please, and to turn all the bread in the house into sandwiches.

[MARY *goes, the* POLICE *following her into the
pantry.*]

Rog, you go out into the laundry and build up a big fire in the stove. Then, when the room's warm and the refreshments are ready, ask our men in the picket line to come in.

DORIS.   [*From the stair*]: Into the house?

RUDI.   That won't really help, John.

JOHN.   It'll help me!

[*Then, hard to* CLEVENGER]:

I'll stand for a good deal of interference, but I will not

have our men saying we do things for the cops that we don't do for them!

[CLEVENGER *shrugs and turns away.*]

Go on, Rog!

[ROGER *goes into the pantry.*]

DORIS.   Well, this settles things as far as I'm concerned!

[*She runs up the stair, calling*]:

Sara! Sara!

[CLEVENGER *turns to* RUDI.]

CLEVENGER.   I can't think what you can do to express your liberal emotions, except to write an editorial in *The Globe*. Don't hesitate to say anything that occurs to you about me that might put you and your brother in a more heroic light.

[RUDI *turns back into the parlor.* CLEVENGER *calls*]:

Ockleford!

[OCKLEFORD *enters from the hall. He wears gloves and coat and carries his hat in his hand.*]

OCKLEFORD.   Right here with the bags, Chief. That was Steve on the phone from the airport just now. Ship's all tuned up and ready to take off.

CLEVENGER.   Did you give my message to Mrs. Garrison?

OCKLEFORD.   She told me to tell you good-bye and she's sorry she's too tired to get up.

CLEVENGER.　Go back upstairs and knock on her door again. Tell her I shan't leave this house till I have seen her. Tell her I'll come up if she doesn't care to come down. And explain that I can arrange to wait through the summer if need be. And certainly until after January 15th.

> [*Needless to say, this last startles* JOHN, *but* OCKLEFORD *goes obediently into the hall and up the stair.* CLEVENGER *turns to* JOHN.]

I've picked up enough around this house this morning to piece out the rest. You needn't be afraid of my spreading rumors. I sympathize too deeply with your predicament.

> [JOHN *bows without answering.*]

You make tools and dies, don't you?

JOHN.　And lathes and drills. All such.

CLEVENGER.　That wouldn't be such a bad war-time business, would it?

JOHN.　We're not at war.

CLEVENGER.　I might say that's unfortunate for you.

> [*A renewed* OUTBURST *from the street.* CLEVENGER *looks out through the parlor.* OCKLEFORD *comes down the stair and into the room. Then, as the* OUTBURST *subsides*]:

OCKLEFORD.　Mrs. Garrison prefers coming down to your going up.

CLEVENGER.　I expected she would. Wait outside till I call you.

> [*Then, as* OCKLEFORD *goes, to* JOHN]:

Will you do me a very great favor, and leave me to talk with your sister-in-law alone? After all, you are entertaining this morning. You should supervise your preparations!

[*Without answer,* JOHN *turns towards the hall, but* SARA, *dressed now in another simple and suitable morning frock, is coming down the stair.*]

SARA. I entirely approve of the coffee and sandwiches, John. Doris is in rather a state. I'd go help her pack if I were you.

[*She comes into the room.* JOHN *goes up the stair.*]

You've fine weather for flying, Jim. After yesterday, almost miraculous.

CLEVENGER. Why didn't you tell me about all this, Sara?

SARA. This what?

[*Then, with a nod towards the window—and a bit too careless*]:

That? Don't let that alarm you.

CLEVENGER. You're cleaned out, aren't you?

SARA. A little tact on your part would have told you that I might be sensitive on the subject. I told you we'd solved our property dilemma.

CLEVENGER. Call this a solution? Reminds me of the Christian Scientist who jumped overboard due to religious scruples against being seasick.

SARA. That's an extreme example.

CLEVENGER. Don't you see this is the end of the world for you, Sara?

SARA. That's just the trouble. It isn't. I'm healthy and I've still got a long time to live.

[*He agrees.*]

CLEVENGER.   With me.

[*She turns, astonished.*]

Marry me, Sara.

[*She gasps.*]

And come with me to Washington.

[*She is properly stunned.*]

SARA.   Now, why should I even consider . . .?

CLEVENGER.   Whatever opinion you may hold of me, and you were pretty clear about that yesterday, I'm just as clear about what I feel for you today. History might have been different if you'd married me! History may still be different if you marry me now!

SARA.   We'll leave history out of this if you don't mind.

CLEVENGER.   I've seen the life you've made for yourself, Sara. All the strength and peace and privacy of it. And I see my own life as I've lived it without you. No center to it, unsettled and frantic. Doesn't that make you the least bit sorry for me?

SARA.   Not enough to prescribe myself as a sedative.

CLEVENGER.   We came together again on a white Christmas. I can't make love to you as a young man could . . .

SARA.   [*Completely off her guard*]: You're not doing badly. That "white Christmas" is rather nice.

[*In spite of herself, the energy of his pleading is stirring her.*]

CLEVENGER.   Sara, I could go into court and take my oath on the President's 15th Century Dutch Bible that you want to say yes!

SARA. Is it conceivable that I'm being tempted?

CLEVENGER. Why not?

[*But a sudden outburst from the* PICKETS *recalls her to her predicament.*]

SARA. I should have to be very sure, shouldn't I?

CLEVENGER. You can be sure of me.

SARA. But I might be using you as a way out. And that wouldn't do at all! Why didn't you go last night?

CLEVENGER. If I had I should have missed what looks like an opportunity this morning.

[*Her eyes flash.*]

Yes, Sara. To open my suit for your heart and hand. Under circumstances which, to my practical mind, make your acceptance . . .

SARA. Look at him with his head up and his tail over the dashboard!

CLEVENGER. You don't like being taken advantage of? Rise above it, Sara. Say to yourself: I'm fond of this man who's dropped back into my life out of the sky and come to care for me the second time . . .

SARA. No.

CLEVENGER. Put on your hat and coat and we'll go get the license.

SARA. [*Crescendo vehemence*]: How can I be sure of what I feel for you when I'm flying in the face of Providence if I don't take you? Why didn't you drop down out of the sky a month ago? I could have seen you clearly and humanly then! With my life before me as it would have been if "all this," as you call it, hadn't happened! I should have seen Joan going out to get married to Martin and Roger following her in a few years and myself left here alone and Mr. Stanford White's architecture getting bigger and bigger and my trips abroad lasting longer and longer and winding up on a world cruise in a white serge suit! I should have seen that my function here was ended and jumped at the chance of a new function with you! But instead you appear just as I've had to give everything up, and offer me a suitcase full of millions and a way out of everything I've got myself into! How can I trust my feeling for you now?

CLEVENGER.   If I say I'll take my chances . . .

SARA.   No, it's no good! Come back in a year! If you really have got to care for me twice, you ought to be able to work yourself up a third time! And if I've made a go of my hat shoppe by then—or whatever I do decide to turn my hand to—I'll be less confused! But it's no good now, with all this around my neck! So go on if you're going and leave me to lie on the bed I've made for myself. Alone.

CLEVENGER.   Oh, Sara, my Sara! You *are* mine, you know! And I'm damned if I let you . . .

> [*Her hand stops him and at the same moment* JOHN *re-appears on the stairs. He carries two bags and the two* CHILDREN, *in their hats and coats, follow him, and* DORIS *brings up the rear and the two in the library are interrupted by a resumption of the family argument.*]

JOHN.   The trouble is . . .

PATIENCE.   But I don't want to go home to the country! You said we could stay with Aunt Sara the whole week!

MICHAEL. [*Practically at the same time*]: Aunt Sara promised to take us to see Pluto tomorrow! And Roger's promised to give me a lesson on skis!

DORIS. Be quiet!

> [*They are down the stair and turning the corner towards the dining room.*]

If you want me to drive myself and your children through this riot . . .

> [*They have disappeared.*]

SARA. [*To* CLEVENGER]: I've got to straighten that out.

> [*Then, pleadingly to him*]:

Will you do something for me? Morgan's out in front with my car waiting for you. Those men of ours won't trouble you, really they won't!

> [*He smiles, but she concludes*]:

Be gone before I come back.

CLEVENGER. Will you do something for me?

SARA. What is it?

CLEVENGER. Kiss me goodbye.

SARA. I don't see why there'd be any harm in that.

> [*She offers her cheek. He takes her in his arms and kisses her hard on the lips. It is not a prolonged motion picture kiss, but he means it and she likes it. Then, still holding her in his arms, he looks down at her.*]

CLEVENGER. Will you remember a farewell message, Sara? That in any choice ever made by any man, between the levelled balances of his interests, there's always a feather's weight to tip the scale. A feather's weight. Will you remember that?

> [*She is puzzled.*]

SARA.   As long as you know what it means.
CLEVENGER.   I do.
SARA.   All right. Goodbye.
CLEVENGER.   Goodbye.

> [*There being nothing more to say, she goes out after* JOHN *and* DORIS. *When he is sure that she is gone, he calls softly*]:

Ockleford!

> [OCKLEFORD *enters.*]

Shut the door.

> [*Then, as* OCKLEFORD *obeys*]:

Come here to me.

> [*His throat is dry, his whole body rigid with the excitement of his resolution.* OCKLEFORD *comes to him.*]

I want you to go down to *The Eagle* and get on the long distance to Curry in New York. I want all the best men taken off what they're doing to round up the families of the captain and crew of the *Farragut*. Pray God that captain left a widow and children! I want interviews and detailed descriptions of each set-up here in my hands within forty-eight hours. That's Wednesday. I want Curry himself out here by Thursday. And he'd better bring Phelps from Washington and Green from Atlanta.

And I want Bronson from Seattle, and some one from San Francisco or Los Angeles, and Bailey from Dallas and Cope from . . .

OCKLEFORD. [*Completely bewildered*]: Chief, what's the idea?

CLEVENGER. We're opening the dike and letting the floods cut loose! This neutrality had to stop sooner or later, Ockleford! I've found my good reason for stopping it a bit sooner!

OCKLEFORD. If we're just taking off for Washington, though . . .

CLEVENGER. Oh, that's all changed! I've been vouchsafed an omen and guidance, Ockleford! I'm staying right here in this house . . .

[*He sits smiling, in* SARA's *big chair.*]

With a feather's weight and an old ermine coat!

[*He leans back happily, singing to himself*]:

> "And when I tell them
>   How wonderful you are!
>   They'll never believe me!
>   They'll never believe me! . . .

[*The curtain, falling, cuts him off.*]

THE FIFTH SCENE

The library again. The tree has been removed. The fire as before. "The Morning Globe" has been left untidily spread out on the sofa. Out of doors the same brightness of brilliant cold.

> [*In the hall,* MARY *is helping* JOAN *to shed cold weather equipment of the best quality.* STEVE *peels off lined trench coat and muffler for himself.*]

MARY. [*As the curtain rises*]: . . . relieved to see you home safely, though I'm sure with a flyer of Mr. Andrews' reputation . . .

> [*A beaming smile for* STEVE *as he enters the library.*]

STEVE. Thank you, Mary. Thank you.

> [*He ambles idly to the sofa, picks up "The Morning Globe" and looks through it without interest.* MARY *drops on her knees to negotiate* JOAN's *galoshes.*]

JOAN. You might tell Mother we're back. She may have worried.

MARY. She's up in her room throwing old trash away and generally getting ready to move out. Mr. Roger he's just drove down to the bakery for more bread to feed the picketeers in the laundry. And there's messages from all your New Year's parties tonight asking will you bring

90

Mr. Andrews along with you, which is only right that you should.

> [*Again the beaming smile for* STEVE. *But* JOAN *has come into the library, leaving* MARY *to dispose of the hats and coats.*]

JOAN. We ought to have waited till tomorrow and flown into the New Year.

STEVE. Flying the old one out wasn't so bad. Don't you think some hot coffee might go pretty well now?

JOAN. Can we have some, Mary?

MARY. Easy, Miss Joan. There's always hot coffee on the stove these days!

> [*She goes into the pantry.* JOAN *is smiling dazedly at* STEVE.]

STEVE. Ears feel funny? That's the change in air pressure coming down. Hold your nose and swallow and push out inside.

> [*She obeys.*]

Did they pop?

JOAN. How did you know my ears felt funny?

STEVE. The way you were acting.

JOAN. That wasn't my ears. I was trying to fix this morning in my memory. That wizened, red-nosed sun that came up and turned the eastern slopes to pink satin. And the sharp, northern look the pines had between the clearings. And those boys we saw skating in front of that schoolhouse. That was like looking down on a picture by Breughel.

STEVE. I'm not artistic. Can't be everything.

> [JOAN *smiles.*]

JOAN.   It seems to me that only two things in the world really matter. The shining space and light we've just been up in . . . and this here.

STEVE.   What here?

JOAN.   Hearth and home it's called.

STEVE.   I never gave 'em a fair trial myself.

JOAN.   They can be pleasant. And painful to lose. I can take hold down here now I've been up there.

STEVE.   I know what you mean. I've often gone up like that. With a hangover. Pumped myself full of good, clean oxygen. Down in ten minutes. Head clear as a bell. That wouldn't be quite your problem.

JOAN.   In principle.

STEVE.   I should be more careful how I put things to you.

JOAN.   How depressing!

STEVE.   Not to me.

JOAN.   Thanks. I'll try being brighter, though.

[*Has a mutual attraction developed? But* MARY *has returned with a breakfast tray which she sets on the cigarette table.*]

STEVE.   Here's coffee.

[MARY *goes.* JOAN *sits down to the tray. But* STEVE, *his eye fixed on her, closes the hall door after* MARY *and comes back to the coffee almost too casually, saying as he does so*]:

I take sugar in mine. Two lumps in summer. Three in winter. That's science. Great heating properties in sugar.

JOAN.   Get a lift with a Camel.

STEVE. I did that. They asked me to and I did it.

[*She has delivered his cup. He sits beside her.*]

JOAN. [*Uncovering the toast plate*]: There's toast, too. Hot, buttered . . .

STEVE. I can eat it.

[*He takes a bite.*]

How do you like your butter? Fresh or salt?

JOAN. Fresh.

STEVE. Salt.

JOAN. I'll tell Anna to . . .

STEVE. No! I'm interested in characteristics, that's all. Been reading up on psychology. Things like different tastes in butter are only skin deep.

[*She finds this touching.*]

JOAN. Then there's no reason why we shouldn't get on very well.

STEVE. There are other things, though.

JOAN. Such as?

STEVE. Which shoe do you put on first?

JOAN. I haven't the faintest notion.

STEVE. That's not the answer.

JOAN. It may not be the answer, but it's the truth.

STEVE. You've got to learn to observe yourself. That's what I'm doing. I find I start everything on the right.

JOAN. I suppose that means you're just constitution-ally right-handed?

STEVE. It might mean that.

JOAN. That's a good thing to find out before it's too late!

STEVE.   You're kidding me.

JOAN.   Have some more coffee.

STEVE.   I've had enough coffee. You have a cigarette.

[*She shakes her head.*]

JOAN.   I don't want to spoil the feel of that good, clean oxygen.

STEVE.   Right.

[*He looks at her somewhat less casually than before.*]

Then tell me what you were thinking about up there.

[*She is surprised.*]

Besides art and nature, I mean.

JOAN.   I was up with one of the world's most famous flyers who's completely unlike anybody I've ever known. What do you suppose I was thinking about?

STEVE.   Me. How?

JOAN.   At your Lost Oasis. In Lhassa. You live half in another element, don't you? You're like a centaur, aren't you?

STEVE.   You keep pulling these on me. What is it?

JOAN.   It *was* in the myths. Half man, half horse. You're half aeroplane.

STEVE.   Two-thirds.

JOAN.   What's the other third?

STEVE.   [*How does he know?*]   Oh, God!

JOAN.   I expect flying's an old story to that lesser third.

STEVE.   It gets monotonous.

JOAN.   Not that last bounce when the wheels really leave? You said planes were meant for fighting. I hate that idea.

STEVE.   You're wrong.

JOAN.   Flight's too beautiful!

STEVE.   So's air fighting beautiful! To shoehorn your-self into one of those little things and go up and look for that other guy and find him with your guns set right there in front of your nose! Man, plane, guns, all one animal then: one bean, one eye!

JOAN.   [*A pause, then, low*]:

"She loved me for the dangers I had passed
And I loved her that she did pity them."

[*Then, at once, because he looks sharply at her,
she is extremely sorry that it slipped out.*]

STEVE.   What's that?

JOAN.   "Othello."

[*She pushes the table from her and rises.*]

I don't know what made me quote it.

STEVE.   Othello. That name strikes a chord. Coon, wasn't he?

JOAN.   He was a Moor. He lived in Venice.

STEVE.   I've been to Venice.

JOAN.   Venice sounds tame for you.

STEVE.   It was all right. It's full of fairies.

JOAN.   Fairies in Venice?

[*She draws back.*]

Oh, you mean . . .

STEVE.   My God!

[JOAN, *feeling foolish, takes refuge in dignity.*]

JOAN.   We don't talk about such things as much as some people.

STEVE.   I didn't know there was a girl left on earth who would have thought I meant anything else!

JOAN.   I'm sure there are plenty!

STEVE.   I told you I'm too free spoken.

JOAN.   It's not your fault if we're a bit old-fashioned in spots.

[STEVE *is suddenly surly.*]

STEVE.   Don't spoil it by apologizing to me, for God's sake!

JOAN.   Steve!

STEVE.   What?

JOAN.   What does get into you?

STEVE.   You wouldn't understand if I told you. I act the way I feel. If you don't like that, this is as good a time as any for saying so.

JOAN.   Really, Steve!

[*She picks up her coat and is moving towards the hall door.*]

STEVE.   Going?

JOAN.   I don't seem to be doing so well here.

STEVE.   Go ahead. Don't let me stop you.

[*She turns back to the door. He speaks without looking at her.*]

Still planning to marry that school teacher, I suppose?

JOAN.   He's not a school teacher any more!

STEVE.   He hasn't changed. And you're finished with him. You must be or you wouldn't have fallen for me.

JOAN.   [*Panic*]: Because I happen to think of a couple of lines of very famous poetry—and they *are* famous whether you've ever heard them or not!

STEVE. I knew what was what this morning up in the plane.

[*An exclamation of dismay from* JOAN.]

Don't worry. You've got me where you want me. In three days without lifting a finger. You say you've never known anybody like me. Well, I've never known anybody like you. I guess that explains it. I could have told you what that remaining third of me is. It's just plain, low-down, gutter-bum male. And you're not the cold-blooded party you think you are.

[*He has gone close to her.*]

JOAN. Please don't.

STEVE. Oh, I'm not proposing to you! I'd ask no girl to marry an aviator. We could get some place, you and I, at that. Want to know what I wish about you? I'll tell you what. I wish to Christ Almighty you weren't a virgin. I'm old-fashioned that way.

[*A sound from* JOAN *but no words will come.*]

Shocked, are you? Sure. But nothing like as shocked as you'd like to be. Well, are you?

[*He takes her in his arms and kisses her soundly. Then he releases her. She backs away unsteadily.*]

Sorry if I was rough. But that's how it is when it really happens. Can't you say something?

[*She shakes her head and goes slowly to pick up her bag where she let it fall on the floor. She totters as she stoops and he picks it up for her.*

> [*She takes it from him and goes unsteadily to the
> hall door.*]

Now listen to me, Joan. You don't want to take this
too . . .

> [*A look from her stops him. Then, opening the
> door, she discovers* JOHN, *where he is shedding
> his coat in the hall.*]

JOHN.   Aren't you looking a bit seedy this morning?
STEVE.   [*Quickly*]: I had her up in the ship to see the
sunrise.

JOHN.   Well, that would account for something.

> [*He has come into the room, apparently weighed
> down by some new burden of care. He slips the
> newspaper into the side pocket of his coat.*]

JOAN.   I'll tell Mother you're here.
JOHN.   You needn't. I've come to see your Uncle Rudi.
JOAN.   I'll tell him.
JOHN.   Mary's already done it.

> [*He sees the paper where it is lying on the sofa.
> He picks it up quickly. Then, with relief*]:

That's the morning paper.

> [*He drops it.*]

Everything seems quiet enough around here.

> [*A look at* STEVE, *intense, and unperceived by*
> JOHN, *and* JOAN *does go out and up the stair.*
> STEVE *is following her.*]

Your father's an extraordinary character. A damned extraordinary character! You may have noticed that.

STEVE.   What's he up to this time?

JOHN.   You don't know?

STEVE.   I never pay much attention.

[JOHN *is drawing his newspaper from his pocket.
But* ROGER *is in from the pantry with* MARTIN
close after him.]

ROGER.   The damnedest thing's happened!

[JOHN *squares off for a blow, but it does not come.*]

MARTIN.   Rog had to go out and buy food for the men
in the picket line . . .

ROGER.   When I got back they'd gone!

MARTIN.   Decamped!

ROGER.   The whole lot of 'em!

STEVE.   They were there on duty when Joan and I
came in!

MARTIN.   And the cops don't know any more than we
do! They saw the men in a huddle, then the whole works
ran off down the street!

ROGER.   Cheering!

[RUDI *is coming down the stair, pajamas, bathrobe and slippers, his hair still towsled.*]

RUDI.   Don't you know that morning papers keep
men up late?

[*But* JOHN *has drawn his paper from his pocket.*]

JOHN.   Mr. Clevenger's *Eagle's* come out with a noon
extra. He's written a little essay on our National Honor.
That isn't staying home any longer. It's going places.

RUDI.   Holy God!

STEVE.   Let's have a look at that, will you?

RUDI.   [*Reading*]: "Honor is not a dead word in a dead language. We are not yet dead to our National Honor. Though we hate war, let us serve notice on these warring nations . . ."

[DORIS *is calling wildly from the front door*]:

DORIS.   Sara! Where *is* everybody?

[*She enters, brandishing another copy of "The Eagle."*]

Have you seen the paper?

RUDI.   If that's what's brought you here . . .?

DORIS.   Oh, not to crow! Truly not to crow! But we ran into Sara's car in front of the post office and . . .

[*She continues her excited chatter ad lib.* SARA *is coming down the stair.*]

MARTIN.   [*Over* DORIS]: "In a deeper sense, these seventeen sailors are all America as Nathan Hale was all America . . .

ROGER.   "Every ton of our fleet, every ounce of powder in our arsenals . . ."

DORIS.   You won't believe what this means to me, but . . .!

SARA.   Doris, where have you come from? John! What are you all . . .!

DORIS.   Oh, Sara, your wonderful friend Mr. Clevenger!

RUDI.   Your wonderful friend's done as much as any man could to involve this country in war!

Doris.   And I love him for it! I just love him for it!
Let her read for herself!

[*She thrusts her paper upon* Sara, *who stands
reading.*]

Every newsboy's got another tagging after him! Handing
out free American flags! And trucks are roaring up and
down all the main streets with banners and radios . . .

John.   And the same show must be going on in every
town where Clevenger's got a paper!

Rudi.   Seattle. Birmingham. Boston. Salt Lake City . . .

John.   Oh, it's National Honor Day for the seventeen
dead American sailor boys of the *Farragut!*

Martin.   What's the President say to this?

Rudi.   He's wondering what in hell to say just as I
am and who'll listen when he says it!

Martin.   [*Reading*]: "The weak can only submit to
humiliation. But we are not weak . . ."

[*He takes the paper apart.* Steve *leaves.* Rudi *is
pacing the room.*]

Doris.   And all we needed was to be told we're not!
And he's told us, thank God! Thank God for France and
England!

[Rudi *stops his pacing to snarl at her.*]

Rudi.   The French sank the *Farragut!!!* This is aimed
straight at the point of France's chin!!!

Doris.   America's awake! That's all I care about!

[Rudi *resumes his pacing, clutching his head, or
the equivalent.*]

ROGER.   I'm going downtown!

[*He goes out, shouting*):

Steve! Wait for me, Steve!

DORIS.   Save room for me! I don't want to miss a minute of this! It almost makes me wish I were a man!

[*She is gone after* ROGER.]

RUDI.   [*A new aspect of it strikes him*]: And the cleverness of it, Holy God! The cold-blooded cleverness of breaking a thing like this in a noon extra! Too late for the evening sheets to come back at him! But just in time to turn New Year's Eve into a patriots' jamboree! Think of the liquor they'll be . . .

SARA.   You're taking this too hard!

RUDI.   Too hard? They may be doing things now that can't be undone! And how am I going to answer this tomorrow? What have I got to say that people aren't sick of hearing? That's the weakness of reason in a time like this! He's got a whole brass band he can play on! I can play one note on a bloody bassoon!

SARA.   But why do you have to rush into print?

RUDI.   You don't expect *The Globe* to take this lying down?

SARA.   How do you know what there is to take?

JOHN.   Good God, Sara!

[MARY *enters*.]

SARA.   I want to be fair!

MARY.   Here's Mr. Anson come to see you, Mr. John.

[BUCK *enters—a very different Buck*.]

BUCK.   It's a great day, Mr. Garrison!

JOHN. Great for what, Buck?

BUCK. Well, for Garrison Tool and Die, among other things! Isn't this just what we needed?

[JOHN *has not thought of this aspect of the situation.*]

Guess you've noticed the boys aren't out there in front any more.

JOHN. [*Horrified*]: They haven't gone back to the plant?

BUCK. Where would you think they'd gone? And they're asking when do they come back to work!

JOHN. Damn! Oh, damn!

[BUCK *turns, leaving* JOHN *stunned, to* RUDI.]

BUCK. It's a great day for the whole, entire American labor movement that's had its bellyful of neutrality!

RUDI. Do you hear that, Sara? Do you want to hear more of what to expect now the lid's off?

SARA. I've heard enough, thanks!

BUCK. [*To* RUDI]: Well, it's you I've come to see. We'll have a big crowd down at Labor Temple tonight and ringing resolutions to put across. And it's them we want to read in *The Globe* tomorrow and no word of any trouble we may have between the local radical element and the strong arm squad we've assembled to handle it!

MARTIN. The A. F. of L. isn't coming out for war, too!

SARA. *The Eagle* said nothing whatever about war!

RUDI. Go back to our old rights of trade it said!

BUCK. Organized labor asks no more than that. Garrison Tool and Die asks no more!

[JOHN *is barely able to control himself.*]

We're for peace and organized labor's for peace! With honor, though, and on a paying basis!

RUDI. It's war he's offering you! Don't kid yourself, Buck! Once we go back to trading and protecting our trade! Once we start writing notes and taking sides . . .!

BUCK. Well, I can't forget the strides organized labor made in the last war!

[*Sensation.*]

MARTIN. Well, that's certainly taking the practical angle!

JOHN. What would you expect? Organized labor doesn't have to fight!

RUDI. And this is the boy who once stumped for Gene Debs and did time with Bill Heywood!

BUCK. We all have our own interests to look after!

SARA. Please! Please don't! I can't . . .

[*All this almost simultaneous and at full voice. MARY has entered.*]

RUDI. Well, I'm going to fight this son of a bitch and his *Eagle* as long as I've got a punch left in me!

MARY. And a young gentleman from your newspaper, Mr. Robert.

RUDI. Who? Where?

[*BURKE enters—sharp young reporter, hat and overcoat.*]

Oh, Burke . . .

BURKE. They thought you might want to hear the low-down, so I . . .

RUDI. I do want to hear it! But I want you down at

the Labor Temple tonight and if any man in that crowd shows the guts to stand up against what is going on today I want him played up for all that's in him tomorrow!

BURKE. [*Delighted*]: Do I take my brass knuckles with me?

RUDI. Take whatever you've got! And come upstairs and tell me the rest while I'm dressing.

[BUCK *is after* RUDI *and* BURKE *as they go towards the stair.*]

BUCK. I never believed I'd hear a Garrison . . .

RUDI. And you get out!

[*He goes up the stair with* BURKE. BUCK *goes towards the front door.*]

SARA. "National Honor." That's a ringing phrase, John.

JOHN. It is that, Sara.

SARA. What's it all going to mean?

JOHN. He's trying to give us a new *Lusitania*, Sara.

SARA. Oh, I don't believe that! The *Farragut* isn't that! We couldn't fight France and England!

JOHN. He must think we could! He's the breed, you know. Mussolini's and Hitler's breed!

SARA. And I don't believe that!

[MARTIN *shakes his head.*]

MARTIN. No. He's too shrewd to think we'd fight with the dictators!

JOHN. Then why does he choose this ship just at this moment, when he could count on the Germans or Japs or Italians to give us another any day?

MARTIN. I don't believe he cares about anything except putting an end to this business depression. If war's the result—well, war's good for business, too. And this *Farragut* at least puts us in a receptive frame of mind, gets us properly de-neutralized so that when the Germans or Japs or Italians do . . .

JOHN. That may well be.

SARA. Men aren't that cold!

MARTIN. Aren't they? You'd be surprised. I believe I'll have a look downtown myself.

[*He goes out.*]

SARA. I could wish I'd lived more in the world and thought more about it. I shouldn't be coming to with such a jolt now.

[*She rises.*]

I'll telephone Jim. He ought to know what it's going to mean.

JOHN. Hasn't he given you any hint of this?

[*She stops on her way out.*]

SARA. No. None.

JOHN. Not in all the hours you've spent with him this week?

SARA. We've talked about . . . Not about world affairs.

JOHN. Doesn't it seem damn peculiar to you that he's stuck on here as he has in this backwater when he had such a move as this up his sleeve?

SARA. He makes the world come to him wherever he is.

JOHN. You know him pretty well, Sara.

SARA.   I know him. Yes.

JOHN.   I should think you might be sorry for that now.

[*A pause. Her answer is a good deal less than assured.*]

SARA.   It's not like you to judge a man without hearing him, John. He wants us to stand up for our national honor again. You may not believe in that, but many men do. Sincere men. Fine, trustworthy men. Not your type or Rudi's, perhaps, but . . .

JOHN.   Not your type, either.

SARA.   Oh, I'm not any type: I . . .

JOHN.   Sara!

[*This is stern and she flinches.*]

SARA.   What?

JOHN.   Why are you trying to make excuses for him?

[*But RUDI and BURKE are coming down the stair.*]

BURKE.   . . . and the streets downtown are all broken out in flags and the drunks are away ahead of New Year's Eve schedule. And there's telegrams coming in from bankers and editors and chambers of commerce and patriotic societies. As fast as he reads 'em he puts 'em out on the wire to the rest of his papers. You'll see the cream of 'em on the front page tomorrow. Under the heading "The Country Behind Us!"

SARA.   Oh, dear!

[*The two have entered the library, RUDI still buttoning his vest and adjusting his tie, though he is also wearing his overcoat and hat.*]

RUDI.   You both want to get this. Burke's my star

reporter on *The Globe*. He's been buying drinks for the boys from Clevenger's *Eagle*.

[*Back to* BURKE]:

Go on, Burke.

BURKE.   He's got a string of mass meetings scheduled for this coming Saturday night in fifteen key cities. He's hired the Arena for the one in this town.

SARA.   But that's hockey night!

RUDI.   It was hockey night. And he's got a competition for recruiting posters coming up. First prize ten thousand bucks. Under the slogan: "Let us be ready when our country calls!" Oh, yeah! And they're making a movie called "The Farragut's Daughter." It seems the captain of the *Farragut* did leave a daughter. She's been through two divorces and runs a pet shop in Atlantic City, but she's going to be Shirley Temple on the screen!

JOHN.   I think I'll ask Mr. Burke to go along, Rudi.

[RUDI *is surprised, as* JOHN *holds the door open for* BURKE. BURKE *goes.* JOHN *closes the door.*]

We've got to get to the bottom of something here.

[*And to* SARA]:

Sara, will you give Rudi and me your authority to ask Mr. Clevenger to move out of this house?

SARA.   Certainly not!

JOHN.   Why not?

SARA.   Why should I?

JOHN.   You *are* trying to find excuses for him, you know. You *are* taking his side against us.

[*She falters. Then, at last,* JOHN's *suspicions come home to* RUDI.]

RUDI. [*Low*]: Holy God!

SARA. [*A deep breath, and she speaks quite simply*]: I'm going to marry him.

[*A pause. RUDI, being unprepared, is rocked. JOHN stands steady.*]

RUDI. I'll have to admit I hadn't thought of that.

SARA. First I thought I would. Then I knew I couldn't. Then I decided I might as well.

RUDI. You can't care for him, though!

SARA. I know it seems strange, but I do.

[*Then*]:

It's only an exceedingly lucky woman who gets a second chance at her second choice.

[*Then*]:

I'd rather not talk about it.

RUDI. But we can't take the Prince of Darkness into the family without some discussion!

[SARA *stiffens, offended.*]

SARA. Better say he's taking me out of the family.

[*This is a blow to both of the brothers.*]

RUDI. I suppose that is what it comes to.

JOHN. You can't expect us to be happy about this, Sara. We wish you every happiness, though.

[*And, for him, the barrier is up already. RUDI, however will not abandon the fight.*]

RUDI. You get used to a family set-up. It's been the three of us for a long time. Now it won't be the three of us any longer. Oh, I don't mean that we've any claim on you!

[*But a new thought occurs.*]

Joan and Roger have, though. Have you thought of them?

SARA.   I'm going to think of myself, if you don't mind.

RUDI.   We were here in this room, the three of us, Christmas Day. Deciding to let the business go to the wall. And you said: "I've a son just at the fighting age whose father was killed in the last war!"

[SARA *bursts out wildly.*]

SARA.   You can't make me believe Jim Clevenger wants us to fight! He's neither a fool nor a criminal, and I refuse to believe until I have to . . .

RUDI.   Please, Sara! We know how you feel.

[*Then*]:

Well, if that's all . . .

[*He goes to the hall door.*]

There's something in making a clean sweep while you're at it. The business, the old house, *The Globe*, now Sara. I'll keep my mind on *The Globe*. Go down and get out the old anti-war rubber stamps and put one more editorial together. Then, in a few days, just at the height of *The Globe's* real reason for being . . . But why look ahead? Maybe Sara's new husband will give me a job!

> [*The last is venomous. He opens the door, to discover* CLEVENGER *in the hall, just in the act of shedding his overcoat. A deadly pause, then* CLEVENGER *enters smiling.*]

CLEVENGER. I take it the liberal front's drawn up against me.

RUDI. Whatever I may think of you as a fellow citizen, Mr. Clevenger, as a fellow publisher I must congratulate you on the effect of the job you've done today. You might have shown more originality, perhaps, but . . .

CLEVENGER. Originality's of no use with mass emotion. The old stand-bys serve better with that. They would have risen to a tenth of what I've given them.

JOHN. It's good of you to find time for us today.

CLEVENGER. Oh, but I've made time for you! I've been busy in your behalf as well as the country's. Don't go, Sara, please. Deceptive though appearances may be, I'm here as the harbinger of glad tidings. "Harbinger"—that sounds like a piece of agricultural machinery, doesn't it? I ring in a golden New Year for you Garrisons. I've just come from your venerable Senatorial banker. He's agreed to extend your company's note indefinitely.

[*Sensation.* MARTIN *has appeared in the hall and now comes into the room to listen intently to what follows.*]

National honor's made a good risk of the tool and die business.

[*The* GARRISONS *are too stunned to comment.*]

I've seen people more grateful for financial salvation.

JOHN. We weren't asking for any kind of salvation from you, Mr. Clevenger.

CLEVENGER. You don't seem to realize that what I've done today would have been done sooner or later by somebody else.

[*But he adds*]:

Too late for you to have profited, however.

RUDI.   We're free to reject our profit, aren't we?

CLEVENGER.   Oh, yes! You can go out on the street and give your business away. Mediæval mystics did that sort of thing. You won't, though.

JOHN.   You feel plenty of contempt for us, don't you, Mr. Clevenger?

CLEVENGER.   Not contempt but compassion! And for all loose thinkers like you! Holding your foggy faith in your smug ideals up as a light for mankind to follow!

RUDI.   When have we ever done any of that? When have we even pretended to be more than we are: a decent American family with faith in the things we've been trained to believe?

JOHN.   Mr. Clevenger must have been trained to believe in them, too! Yet he finds us ridiculous . . .

CLEVENGER.   Well, I ask you! Is there a more ludicrous figure on earth than the man whose convictions are such he can't fight to uphold them?

[*Now* RUDI *really explodes.*]

RUDI.   We've got no convictions that keep us from fighting you! I'll fight you as long as I've got a punch left in me!

[*A chuckle from* CLEVENGER. RUDI *continues to* JOHN]:

We'll find a way out of this! He thinks he's trapped us! He hasn't! We'll find a way out without hauling our colors down!

JOHN.   What way? He has saved the business. And the house and *The Globe* with it. We can't throw 'em away or get rid of 'em even. And what would it prove if we could? A solemn, Sunday-school gesture! Nothing more.

> [*He sits on the sofa, accepting his fate. But kind-liness comes to* CLEVENGER, *and he sits beside* JOHN *to administer consolation.*]

CLEVENGER.   I see nothing for you to be downcast about. We can all of us use salvation these days. Why, day before Christmas, at my Idaho paper mill, I watched a small army of out-of-work lumberjacks attack my company stores. And they weren't driven off till my guards had killed twenty-three of them! How long can we let that kind of thing go on?

MARTIN.   Property, eh?

CLEVENGER.   [*Surprised*]: What's that?

MARTIN.   I said "property."

> [*Then*]:

Didn't John and I tell you, Sara? We're walking ourselves right into a world war to look after a mess of property.

CLEVENGER.   Aren't you rather jumping at conclusions? We're not at war yet.

MARTIN.   No. But you're ready to take your chances on war to look after your property.

CLEVENGER.   [*Outraged*]: Not mine! Yours, too, if you've got any! Everybody's! Whether it's the circulation of newspapers for me or a widow's income from a family business for Sara . . .

MARTIN.   Oh, sure, sure! Liberals own property, too.

> [*Then, to* JOHN]:

What are you going to do about it, though? Sit tight? Keep on seeing both sides of the question and getting no-

where? Or will you come down to the Labor Temple with
me and stand up with the Reds and see what we can start?

> [*The* GARRISON *brothers are mutually dismayed,
> but* SARA *goes quickly to* MARTIN.]

SARA.   You're not going there!

MARTIN.   I don't want to go there. I'm likely to get
the daylights beaten out of me! But I'm damned if I see
anywhere else to go!

RUDI.   Holy God, he's gone Communist on us!

SARA.   I was afraid somebody would before we got
through!

MARTIN.   Maybe I have.

> [*He points to* CLEVENGER.]

I've noticed extremes breed each other in this life! But
you've got to fight dogma with dogma! And this is the
dogma of property here! Call it patriotism! Call it any
damn thing! Well, history's always turned its corners on
dogma and saved reason for the straightaways between!
If we're past the choice between fighting or not, I mean to
fight to the root of the matter.

RUDI.   What root, for God's sake?

MARTIN.   Clevenger's root, for God's sake! Property,
for God's sake!

JOHN.   You're talking like a damn fool!

MARTIN.   Well, what is to blame for this if property
isn't? The business, *The Globe*, Sara's house, the whole
cock-eyed . . .

SARA.   There's no good in violence, Martin!

MARTIN.   Clevenger's rather won me around to thinking there may be.

> [*He turns back to* RUDI *and* JOHN.]

You two may be right to let things ride. My patience has damn well run out on me. Clevenger wants results! Well, I want 'em, too! I suppose this washes this family up on me.

[*He turns back to* SARA.]

I'm sorry for that. I'm fond of this family.

[*He goes quickly into the hall and out of sight, snatching his coat and hat as he passes the table.* SARA *turns after him, then desperately back to the Garrison brothers. But* RUDI *is already on his way after* MARTIN.]

RUDI.   Now, you don't want to do anything you'll be sorry for, Martin . . .

[*And* JOHN *follows* RUDI *into the hall.*]

JOHN.   Keep your shirt on, Martin! You've always been level-headed and . . .

SARA.   [*At the same time*]: Stop him! You've got to stop him!

[*And, unmindful even of the slam of the front door, she turns wildly on* CLEVENGER.]

That boy! I brought him up! Here in this house as one of this family! You've driven him out! What is this horrible thing you're trying to do?

CLEVENGER.   Nothing, I tell you, that some one else wouldn't have done!

SARA.   You don't *know* that! *You* needn't have done it! You did ask me for guidance!

CLEVENGER.   And you gave it.

[*She is stunned.*]

SARA.   I gave it? For this?

CLEVENGER.   I saw those pickets in front of this house and understood why you'd called me your "way out!" There's always a feather's weight, remember, Sara! I did choose between delay and action then, because I could, then, save your pride with your property and clear away the barrier between us!

SARA.   You fool! You blind, uncomprehending ninny! What do you call this that's between us now?

CLEVENGER.   There's nothing between us now!

SARA.   Oh, isn't there!

CLEVENGER.   You love me, Sara!

SARA.   I know what I am to you, though! You were on your way to robbing the mint and you picked a penny out of a blind man's plate and I'm the penny! You've wound your cords 'round and around this house . . .

CLEVENGER.   Good stout cords! No idealistic weak spots in 'em!

SARA.   Now you're twisting 'em into a hangman's noose for me!

CLEVENGER.   Step on the trap, Sara! It won't be painful!

SARA.   How can you talk about any of that now? How can you ask me to think about that now? I can only see that Joan may be standing where I stood when Paul went to France! And that Roger may be just where his father was! That's what you've put between us now, you dolt! I was a woman in love with a man this morning! Look at me now! I'm the Great American Mother!

[*He laughs delightedly.*]

How can you laugh! You've a son of your own, Jim! Have

you no thought for him? Oh, I didn't know I could ever be afraid of you but I *am* afraid of you now!

[*He stops laughing abruptly. He goes to her.*]

CLEVENGER.   Of me, Sara? Not of the world as it is in spite of you? It's odd, though, your saying that just then. Because I've always been the least bit afraid of you. And I'm not afraid of you now.

[*Her gesture waves him away. She sits, dismally, in her big chair.*]

I'll be going now. I've done what I had to do here.

SARA.   I hope so. I hope so.

[*He goes out, leaving her staring into the dark portent of the future. The curtain falls.*]

THE SIXTH SCENE

[*The curtain rises again immediately.*]

The lamps are lighted and the curtains drawn. The doors to both hall and parlor stand open.

> [CLEVENGER *sits by the fire, his after-dinner coffee and a glass of brandy on the cigarette table in front of him. He sips first one, then the other, and reads a sheaf of telegrams which* OCKLEFORD *hands him. Some of these he drops into a waste-paper basket placed alongside the table. Others he piles neatly beside his coffee cup. The* RADIO *is being operated in the parlor. The sound is a confusion of patriotic band selections, choruses and oratory, one shifted brutally into another.*]

OCKLEFORD. Can't complain of the radio program, Chief. Wonderful how the commercial hours took such quick advantage. Of course it's as much to their interest as ours. And there's no royalty charge for patriotic material.

> [*But* JOHN *and* DORIS *enter from the parlor, he dressed as before; she very much got up for the evening and with quite a touch of red, white and blue about her costume.*]

DORIS. I do think it's mean of you!
JOHN. I'm just not in the mood for parties tonight.
DORIS. Not in the mood? And the most thrilling New

118

Year's Eve that's ever been? You'd better learn to get in the mood, my dear! And stay in it! If you don't want everybody turning against you! Everybody but your beloved Rudi and Sara, that is!

[*And she appeals*]:

You tell him, Mr. Clevenger! Here we've come in from the country, with four parties to go to and . . .

JOHN.   Don't bother Mr. Clevenger. I'll go up and dress.

> [*He starts towards the door. From the* RADIO *in the parlor another outburst of patriotic oratory which is quickly dimmed by whoever is operating the volume control.* JOHN *turns to* CLEVENGER *and* OCKLEFORD.]

I'll say this for you, Mr. Clevenger. At least you don't make any pretense of believing that hogwash yourself.

> [CLEVENGER'S *eyes flash a signal to* OCKLEFORD, *who draws himself up.*]

OCKLEFORD.   The Clevenger papers never ask the public to believe anything they don't believe themselves. That's a policy almost amounting to a motto.

> [*Disgusted and angry,* JOHN *turns and goes up the stair.*]

DORIS.   I just can't wait for the Red Cross Drive to start. And all those more intimate little committees!

> [*And, over her shoulder as she leaves*]:

You don't know about the spy I caught last time!

> [*She goes into the parlor, passing* CALLORY *as he enters, dressed for the evening.*]

CALLORY.   [*Over the radio, which takes a sudden crescendo spurt*]: You're the only one I haven't said good night and Happy New Year to, Mr. Clevenger. My heart, as both banker and patriot, is pouring out thanks for the job you've done today! Not that you aren't hearing that pretty generally.

> [*A gesture towards the telegrams in* CLEVENGER'S *hand.*]

Sara's concerned for her children. That's not unnatural. I've advised her to turn to you for help with them.

> [MARY *enters with the regulation after-dinner tray of ice water, glasses, whiskey and soda. She sets the tray on a side table and goes.* CLEVENGER *rises.*]

CLEVENGER.   I'm glad you did, Senator. And I can assure you as a friend of this family's that those children of Sara's have never been safer. As for the boy, I'm ready to guarantee that he won't be permitted to get himself into danger, no matter how he may beg!

> [STEVE *chooses just this moment to enter,* ROGER *following.* STEVE's *manner is both wary and impudent,* ROGER's *breathless with excitement.*]

STEVE.   How busy are you?
CLEVENGER.   [*Surprised*]: Did you want something?
STEVE.   Any idea of when we'll be pushing on?
CLEVENGER.   On?
STEVE.   To points East.

> [SARA *has followed the boys in. She is dressed now in a simple but most beautiful house evening frock.*]

CLEVENGER. [*A smile for* SARA.]: I don't think the most blatant optimism would justify my leaving for a few days yet.

STEVE. Then you'll have to get yourself some new flying arrangements.

[*The briefest pause, then*]:

CLEVENGER. Really? Why?

STEVE. Because if I don't get to New York some time tomorrow I don't catch the boat on Saturday.

CLEVENGER. What boat?

STEVE. I forget the name. It's one of the French ones.

[*This really stops* CLEVENGER. *Then he turns, holding his telegrams out to* OCKLEFORD.]

CLEVENGER. We'll answer these in the morning. The rest don't matter. That's all for now.

[OCKLEFORD *goes, replacing the wastepaper basket by the desk on his way.*]

And good night to you, Senator Callory. And let me thank you for what *you've* done today, in Sara's name.

CALLORY. I don't want any thanks. My old friend's business, Sara's security, this house where I've spent fifty Christmas Days . . .

CLEVENGER. And a Happy New Year, Senator . . .

[*And he has got the* SENATOR *on his way. Then he returns to* STEVE.]

Now where do you think you're going on a French boat?

STEVE. [*Steady as a rock*]: To Paris. Where the old Lafayette boys went in 1915. We new Lafayettes like French food and blue uniforms, too.

[CLEVENGER'S *eyes narrow.*]

CLEVENGER. You new Lafayettes?

STEVE. That's me. And nine others just as good as I am, only they haven't had the breaks I've had. Must have dropped two hundred bucks on the long distance this afternoon. Don't worry, Mrs. Garrison. I went to the hotel.

[*Then, back to* CLEVENGER]:

The old Lafayettes had two lion cubs for mascots. We've got everything set but the cubs and I'll have them tomorrow.

ROGER. I'll bet you will, Steve!

[*Startled*, SARA *turns her attention to her son.*]

CLEVENGER. What did you expect me to say to this?

STEVE. That's a question I haven't thought about much. All I know is I'm washed up on pushing you around. I'd as soon drive a milk route as do your kind of flying.

[CLEVENGER *controls his anger.*]

CLEVENGER. Do I have to remind you that you're under contract to me?

STEVE. [*His most impudent grin*]: Don't I always give the other party his chance to tear up the contract before I tell him to go to hell and sue?

CLEVENGER. I signed that contract because I wanted you with me. It isn't unnatural that I should want my son with me.

STEVE. And it isn't unnatural that you never thought about it till I'd made damn good publicity of my name!

CLEVENGER. I might remind you, then, of an Act of Congress to keep our boys out of foreign armies.

STEVE. That law's a dead letter. You killed it today.

CLEVENGER. You'll lose your citizenship!

STEVE. I never voted yet.

CLEVENGER. I'll sue you! I'll slap a summons on you at the dock! You'll never get on that boat!

STEVE. And I'll tell the papers how you stopped me because you want us fighting on Hitler's side and what do your Jewish readers say to that? No answer. I guess everything's covered.

[*He is going into the hall.*]

I'll pack my stuff now. I'm going tonight so I've got to pack my stuff now.

[*He is on his way up the stair.* CLEVENGER *turns desperately to* SARA.]

SARA. You see, Jim? It's all happening all over again.

[CLEVENGER *turns and goes up the stair, calling*]:

CLEVENGER. You think you've had the last word, young man, but I'm not done yet! I am your father! And there are some things a boy owes his father! I don't expect either loyalty or obedience from you . . .

STEVE. That's lucky for you, because you wouldn't get 'em! They wouldn't be in your line anyway!

[*A door slamming above cuts them off. But* SARA's *interest is on* ROGER, *who closes the hall door and turns uneasily towards the window.*]

ROGER. It's snowing again.

SARA. Is it?

ROGER. The paper said snow. A big storm moving East. Put a kind of a damper on the excitement, won't it?

SARA. [*She sits in her big chair again.*] If it would

snow all over the country. . . . Steadily, now, for weeks and weeks. And bury all the excitement under a thick, wet blanket.

ROGER.   You don't think I'm falling for it?

SARA.   No!

ROGER.   Steve's got the right idea. Be hard-boiled about it. What is there in it for him, Steve says. I don't know, though, which is the right way to go at it. To fall for the bunk and put your heart into it, or Steve's way, just for the hell of it.

[*He has to recover himself.*]

If you're going at it at all.

[SARA *has grown very wary with him.*]

SARA.   We're not at war yet.

ROGER.   I'm selfish enough to hope we don't go to war.

SARA.   What makes you call that selfish?

ROGER.   You wouldn't want people calling me a slacker?

SARA.   There's only one thing that could make you a slacker, Rog. That would be staying out for any reason except your own conviction.

ROGER.   You're not asking me what I'm going to do.

SARA.   To do? What about?

ROGER.   When . . . *if* we go into this war.

SARA.   Do you want me to ask you?

ROGER.   Yes, I think I do.

SARA.   I thought you might. That's why I thought I wouldn't.

ROGER.   Putting it up to me, are you?

SARA.   I don't see any one else to put it up to.

ROGER. Don't worry. I'll stick by our guns.

[*He laughs.*]

Well, not "guns."

[*Then*]:

That word "pledge," though. It's a lousy, Sunday-school word!

> [*He gives up and opens the hall door to leave. Once again voices—now distantly muffled—are audible above stairs:* CLEVENGER *and* STEVE *still at it.*]

CLEVENGER. [*Off-stage*]: When I lay down a policy in my papers, I consider it my son's duty to subordinate his weakness for morbid excitement . . .

STEVE. [*Off-stage, at the same time*]: Forget it! Dry up! Go sell your papers some place else!

[*Then, riding him down*]:

I'm starting for Paris tonight!

> [ROGER *closes the door, his resolution revived.*]

SARA. That sounds like Steve's round.

ROGER. [*Low*]: I want to go with Steve, Mother.

SARA. [*Very cool*]: Straight off to France?

ROGER. A man of my age isn't satisfied just to read about life!

SARA. [*A deep breath, then*]: I can understand that. I might get Mr. Clevenger to send you over for one of the papers.

ROGER. That wouldn't be the real thing.

SARA. Want the real thing, do you?

ROGER. If a man doesn't get into the real thing some time!

SARA.   You've still got a few years, you know.

ROGER.   A few years of what? We've got the business back again. Four years of college. Forty of the business. What's that add up to against learning to fly? If we do go in, wouldn't you like me all trained and ready to take my part as my father did?

SARA.   You're terribly like your father at the moment.

ROGER.   Am I?

SARA.   Terribly!

ROGER.   Why put it that way?

SARA.   If I mean it that way?

ROGER.   You loved my father!

SARA.   I love you.

ROGER.   That isn't fair! In a year and a half I'll be twenty-one! I'm a man!

SARA.   And you've got to be manly and fall in line with . . .

> [JOHN—*now in his dinner coat—enters from the hall. The opening of the door admits a fresh burst of the argument above stairs.*]

CLEVENGER.   [*Off-stage*]: You'll start nowhere to-night! You'll stay here in this house! That plane's my property!

STEVE.   [*Off-stage, at the same time*]: If you scream that way you'll burst another blood vessel in your eye and get out of this room and leave me to pack!

JOHN.   What in God's name goes on between those two upstairs?

SARA.   We'll let them fight it through to a knock-out and you referee this bout between Roger and me?

ROGER.   Now, none of that!

SARA.   Let your Uncle John take you on!

[*To* JOHN]:

The war fever's caught up with the Garrison family, John!

ROGER.   I don't give a hoot in hell for my Uncle John!
All he does is spout about the horrors of war!

JOHN.   You don't believe in 'em?

ROGER.   I'm sick of hearing about 'em! You men of
your age had your war! This is *our* war! Maybe you're
right about yours! What do I want to do that's so different
from . . .

> [*But* JOAN *is down the stair and into them—the
> tumult above stairs still continuing—before he
> can finish.*]

JOAN.   [*Wild*]: You've got to stop him!

JOHN.   Stop whom?   } [*Together*]
SARA.   Joan, what's the matter?

ROGER.   You talking about Steve, too?

JOAN.   He's going away and I can't get at him because
that awful father's in there with him and I haven't got
any time! Do something, Mother!

> [*She is very close to tears.*]

ROGER.   My God, if she hasn't fallen in love with Steve!

JOAN.   What if I have? What's it to you if I have?

ROGER.   It's O.K. with me! It's great!

SARA.   [*Stunned*]: I wasn't prepared for this! John,
will you please . . .?

> [*She motions him out.*]

And see that no one gets in here till I . . .

ROGER.   But you haven't told me yet what I can . . .

JOHN.   Your problems can wait!

ROGER.   They can't wait! Steve's leaving!

JOHN.   They're going to wait!

[*He has* ROGER *with him out in the hall and the door closed after them. Meanwhile* SARA *has seated* JOAN *on the sofa beside her.*]

SARA.   What is it you want me to do?

JOAN.   Stop him! Stop him!

SARA.   But I'm thinking of Martin! You might think about him!

JOAN.   I can't think about Martin! I won't think about him! Steve's going away! I can't let him go, Mother! You've got to stop him! You're being no help at all!

[*And* SARA *sees that her daughter's case requires even more tact and wariness than her son's.*]

SARA.   Joan, darling, I can't just pull this straight like a string trick! What's he want to do?

JOAN.   Go away!

SARA.   It's no fun having a husband away at war.

JOAN.   But he doesn't want to get married!

SARA.   Did he suggest any alternative?

JOAN.   That's as far as we got.

SARA.   Well, that's somewhere.

[*And she becomes more hopeful.*]

Isn't it, though, a sign that he may not be quite as serious as you are?

JOAN.   He loves me! I don't care about being married! I can't let him go! Can't you talk to him, Mother?

SARA. What can I say to him? Except that I shan't be sorry to see him go? And I do think you should talk to Martin before . . .

JOAN. Martin isn't here and I haven't got any time! And why can't you try to help instead of objecting! And making things harder for me and . . .

[*She is very near breaking.*]

SARA. But it's nothing unusual for a girl to love two men at once! I've done it often! It's complicated, I know! But it doesn't mean that you don't love Martin as much as . . .

[*Then* JOAN *does explode.*]

JOAN. What do you know about me or the way I feel? You've forgotten what it means to be in love! If you ever knew!

SARA. I wish I had never known! Because then I should know what to do about this!

JOAN. You don't know Steve! You've never seen him in his plane!

SARA. You wouldn't be living with him in his plane.

JOAN. I'll never live anywhere with him if he gets away! You will talk to him, won't you?

SARA. I wish I knew what to say!

[*She calls*]:

Rog! Rog, come in here a . . .

[ROGER *opens the door.*]

Will you ask your friend Steve Andrews to come down?

[ROGER *calls up the stairs.*]

ROGER.   Steve!

STEVE.   [*From above and muffled*]: What?

ROGER.   Come down here, will you? My mother wants you.

[*A pause, then*]:

STEVE.   Right.

SARA.   [*To* JOAN]: You can't stay here, you know!

JOAN.   I may never see him again if I don't!

[STEVE *is coming down the stairs.*]

SARA.   But I cannot stand your young man up on the carpet to ask him if his intentions are honorable with you sitting there looking as dishonorable as . . .

JOAN.   [*On her feet*]: He's coming now!

SARA.   Oh, Joan, my dear Joan, he isn't the first hero to ride off to the wars!

[STEVE *enters.* ROGER *follows, sneakingly, and closing the hall door after him.* SARA *rises.*]

I asked you to come down here, Mr. Andrews.

[*A movement of protest from* STEVE.]

I'm sorry, but I can't call you anything more intimate and get through what I have to say. Whatever that is.

[*Then, to* JOAN]:

Joan, won't you please . . .?

[JOAN *sits decisively.*]

Well, if you don't find this embarrassing, I don't see why I should!

[*Then, back to* STEVE]:

You've succeeded in causing quite an emotional disturbance in this house. Now you're off to France, wreathed in palms of glory, to lead a flying squadron into battle, in spite of the fact that something seems to have happened between you and Joan. I'm interested to hear any helpful observations you may have to offer.

STEVE. I don't think of any.

SARA. You love Joan?

STEVE. Yes.

SARA. That's serious, is it?

STEVE. It is with me.

SARA. And still you're going away to France tonight?

STEVE. She says herself I'm two-thirds aeroplane. I couldn't love anybody enough to give up what I can't help doing.

SARA. Thank God for the one-track mind!

JOAN. [*To* STEVE]: You know I wouldn't want you to give it up!

SARA. [*Overwhelmed*]: Oh, dear, oh, dear! You should have taken her to Lhassa with you!

STEVE. I didn't know her then.

SARA. Do you want to say anything to her alone before you go?

STEVE. What?

SARA. Well, I don't like to make suggestions, but . . . "Good-bye."

STEVE. Better not.

[*A sob, just one, from* JOAN.]

SARA. That may be, too.

[*To* ROGER]:

Rog, will you tell Morgan he's wanted to take Mr. Andrews to the station? And get his bags down?

ROGER.   Now? Right off?

SARA.   The sooner the better. Much the better, I think.

STEVE.   Only it's the airport, not the station, if that's O.K.

ROGER.   Flying in this snow?

STEVE.   I've flown in worse. I get carsick on trains.

[ROGER *goes, troubled, by the pantry door.* SARA *holds out her hand to* STEVE.]

SARA.   You can say good-bye to me at any rate. I've precious little use for what you're up to, but that doesn't blind me to your other attractions!

STEVE.   Thank you.

[*He takes her hand.*]

Good-bye.

[*But* JOAN *is on her feet.*]

JOAN.   Don't take Rog with you . . .

SARA.   He's not taking Rog!

JOAN.   Take me!

SARA.   Joan!

[*He is startled.*]

STEVE.   Would you want to come with me?

JOAN.   I shan't ever see you again if you don't take me!

SARA.   Joan! My dear Joan!

[*Then to* STEVE]:

If you've any sense of anything, Mr. Andrews . . .!

STEVE.   You can leave this to me, Mrs. Garrison.

JOAN.   Why do you listen to her when she's just said she's against you? I'm not against you and you don't want to give me up! And I promise to keep out of the way in New York and not even to try talking you out of sailing!

SARA.   Joan, you don't know what you're saying!

[ROGER *comes down the stair with* STEVE's *bag, leaves it in the hall and comes into the room.*]

JOAN.   I don't care what I'm saying! Do you expect me to let the man I love go off to war and sit back and say nothing? And he loves me! And I'd follow him to Paris if he'd let me! Just to be there and see him when he gets leave and . . .

ROGER.   You with a lot of us flyers in Paris?

JOAN.   You keep out of this, Rog!

SARA.   I won't have any more of this, Joan!

JOAN.   He might not come back! Father didn't! You ought to understand! I never thought you'd let me down!

SARA.   I'm not letting you down! This is what happened to me with your father! And it's not going to happen to you if I can help it!

JOAN.   I don't care about that! I don't care!

ROGER.   [*At the same time*]: You *can't* help it! You may keep Joan here, but you can't keep me!

SARA.   You'll do as your legal guardians say for a while yet!

[STEVE *is already on his way, but* JOAN *goes after him.*]

JOAN.   Not yet! You can't go yet!

[*Voices*—RUDI's *and* JOHN's—*are audible in the hall from the front door.*]

STEVE.   Joan! For God's sake! I do love you! You're right about that! And I'll come back if you'll wait for me . . .

SARA.   Will you go, if you're going?

STEVE.   Right.

> [*Going, he runs into* JOHN *and* RUDI *and they enter talking excitedly and both together. They stop to watch* STEVE *leave.*]

JOAN.   [*A wild cry*]: Steve! No!

SARA.   Joan, I'm ashamed of you!

> [*She has gripped* JOAN's *arm. The door is heard to slam. Then*]:

JOAN.   Let me go, please.

> [SARA *releases her. She goes weakly up the stair,* SARA *and both brothers looking after her. The* RADIO *in the parlor has been for some time broadcasting a military march. Now it switches suddenly to a mellifluous female voice in a recitation.* SARA *turns listening, disgusted, until she hears the words:* " 'Shoot, if you must, this old gray head, but spare your country's flag,' she said." *This is very much too much for her and she is charging the parlor.*]

JOHN.   I'm sorry, Sara, but . . .

SARA.   [*Distracted*]: What is it now?

RUDI.   Martin's got himself hurt.

> [SARA *turns. The radio recitation continues.*]

JOHN.   He did go to that labor meeting. He did stand

up and the Reds did get behind him and Buck's strong arm squad . . .

SARA.   [*Loud at the parlor*] : Shut that damn thing off!

[*Then, as silence falls on the radio*] :

Is he badly hurt?

[DORIS *enters*.]

DORIS.   Really, Sara, I don't think you've any . . .

[*But* RUDI *cuts her off*.]

RUDI.   Not badly. No. They took a few stitches in his head, that's all.

SARA.   And Joan . . .

[*Then*] :

I'll go to him. Where is he?

JOHN.   That's it. He's locked up in a cell in the city jail.

[*This is a jolt but* SARA *controls herself*.]

SARA.   I'll go to him there.

RUDI.   I wouldn't. It's a nasty place. Stinks of creosote. The thing is to get him out.

SARA.   Can't you do that?

RUDI.   You don't know the temper of this town tonight. I'm not the respected citizen I was. And tomorrow's a holiday and he won't even get his hearing till day after. So I thought. . . . Well, I came here thinking . . .

DORIS.   That you'll have to turn to Mr. Clevenger.

[*A pause, then*] :

JOHN.   Again?

RUDI.   He really does own the police, you know.

[SARA *goes to the stair and calls up.*]

SARA.   Jim! Will you come down here a minute, Jim?

> [*A strained pause:* SARA *immobile,* DORIS *trium-*
> *phant, the Garrison brothers miserable. Then,*
> *suddenly,* RUDI *turns to make himself a whiskey*
> *and soda and* CLEVENGER *is coming down the*
> *stair.*]

CLEVENGER.   I'm sorry, Sara, for the disturbance Steve and I . . .

[*He looks around him.*]

Or is this something else?

SARA.   We've had our first war casualty already, Jim. Martin Holme's been saying what he believes and got himself beaten up and arrested for it. Will you get him out of jail for me?

[CLEVENGER *smiles, then*]:

CLEVENGER.   You're sure jail isn't a good place for him? He'll only get himself into more trouble, you know.

SARA.   I thought Paul's death had cured me of hero worship. I'm not sure I'm cured.

CLEVENGER.   I'll get on the phone to *The Eagle.*

[*He goes out.*]

RUDI.   Can you trust him, Sara?

[*A look, then* SARA *follows* CLEVENGER *out.*]

JOHN.   [*To* RUDI]: Can we trust Sara? [RUDI *is shocked.*] Not to let him put anything over on her, I mean.

RUDI.   We might just stand around.

[*They follow* SARA *out.*]

DORIS.   Of course if young men will try to stand out against the inevitable. I've always said Martin was his own worst enemy. Don't you make any such mistake, will you, Roger?

> [*She goes into the parlor where the* RADIO *presently resumes martial music.* ROGER *lifts two desperate hands to heaven. Then* JOAN *is coming furtively down the stair. She wears her ermine coat and carries a small dressing case. She enters the room.*]

JOAN.   Lend me your car?
ROGER.   Where do you think you're going?
JOAN.   I've packed a bag.

[*She shows it.*]

ROGER.   You'll be sorry!
JOAN.   Will you lend me your car? I haven't got any time!
ROGER.   Pipe down!

[*Then, as he is producing his car keys*]:

You'll be sorry, I tell you.

JOAN.   [*Frightened, obsessed, pathetic*]: You can come if you like.

ROGER.   You know I'd like, all right.

JOAN.   Will you come? Or had you rather stay here in this . . . this . . .

[*She can find no name for such stuffiness.*]

Roger.   Jesus!

[*She takes the keys from him.*]

Joan.   Well . . .

[*She starts towards the pantry door.*]

Roger.   Hold it. My coat's right here in the . . .

[*He follows her to the hall, where she stands waiting quietly in the open pantry door. He disappears and re-appears at once, struggling into his coat.*]

I ought to pack a bag. I ought to take . . .

Joan.   There isn't time for that! Do you want to miss him?

Roger.   No. But it's a hell of a thing to go to war in a dinner coat!

Joan.   I'm taking my ermine.

[*They slip out through the pantry door. The* Radio *swells. The curtain falls.*]

THE SEVENTH SCENE

[*The curtain rises again immediately.*]

The lamps and fire as before.

> [SARA *stands at the window, the curtain drawn back to show the blizzard out-of-doors.* JOHN *and* RUDI *sit side by side on the sofa. The bottle of whiskey is nearly empty on the coffee table before them and three or four empty pints of White Rock stand on the floor.*]

RUDI.   [*As the curtain rises*]: I can't help feeling sorry for myself. Life may begin at forty for professional grandfathers but panic begins at forty for professional writers. The day comes when you have to admit the piece you've just written took twice as long as it would have a few years before.

> [MARY *enters from the pantry with a tray of coffee—large thermos pot and large cup—which she sets on a small table. She moves the table to place it beside* SARA's *big chair.* RUDI *continues throughout.*]

And you buy a new pencil sharpener to speed things up and pin your ideas on the wall so you won't forget 'em. Or will forget where you read 'em! And what you need is a professional home! Where you can be sure of print for a few years longer. Have you ever known an ex-liberal editor?

> [*He shudders and empties his glass.*]

SARA.   [*To* MARY]: What time's it getting to be?

MARY.   Close on half past eleven.

SARA.   Miss Joan's still quiet?

MARY.   As a mouse, Mrs. Garrison.

SARA.   That's all, Mary, thank you. You can go to bed.

MARY.   Good night, Mrs. Garrison.

SARA.   Good night.

> [MARY *leaves.* SARA *goes to her big chair, sits and pours herself a cup of black coffee.*]

RUDI.   If they want to fight, all *The Globes* in the world can't stop 'em. But I can have a lot of fun trying to. Oh, no! I couldn't have given up *The Globe!*

> [*He is mixing another drink.* JOHN *sweetens his.*]

JOHN.   *The Globe's* saved now. And the house and the business with it. And Sara's marrying Clevenger.

> [SARA's *head comes up. She frowns.*]

SARA.   We agreed not to talk about Sara and Clevenger.

RUDI.   Right.

JOHN.   The truth about us is: we're afraid of Clevenger. He makes the world as men have messed it up more valid than the world as it ought to be. That's part of the power of evil in men like him. They can make what's sound and good seem senseless folly. And men like you and me sound like solemn fools.

SARA.   Have another drink.

RUDI.   You have one.

SARA.   Coffee's my vice, thanks.

JOHN.   You're waiting up for Clevenger to come back from the airport?

SARA.   Why not wait up? It *is* New Year's Eve. And I'm at least interested to see if he brings Steve back with him.

[JOHN *laughs.*]

JOHN.   I don't want to be nasty, but I did enjoy his howls when he heard Steve was gone.

RUDI.   Now *I* want to forget about Sara and Clevenger.

JOHN.   Right.

RUDI.   I think I'll marry my girl.

JOHN.   You'd better go out and get yourself some air.

RUDI.   In this snow? I'll open my window . . .

[*He illustrates the size of the opening with thumb and forefinger.*]

But that's as far as I'll go.

[JOHN, *rising, knocks over one or two of the White Rock bottles.*]

JOHN.   I haven't got so I knocked things over for years.

RUDI.   I can knock anything over when I'm tight. Including women.

SARA.   Really, Rudi!

[*This is the tolerant boredom which drink induces in the sober.*]

You ought both of you to be ashamed of yourselves!

RUDI.   Why?

SARA.   Oh, I don't know. The state of the world for

one thing. Poor Martin upstairs in bed with his broken head.

[*A shrug. It is all too distressing.*]

RUDI. Martin had the wrong idea. Too violent.

JOHN. If I believed property really is to blame . . .

SARA. The evils of property are apt to be clearer to those who don't own any.

[*But* JOHN, *being troubled again, sits to pour just one more small one.*]

JOHN. We don't seem to be very clear about things, though, do we?

SARA. There's this much merit in confusion: if you stay confused you'll never be orthodox.

[JOHN *sees her point. So does* RUDI.]

RUDI. The truth about us is we're both in love with you, Sara.

[SARA *smiles. He continues to* JOHN]:

I've always known that. I asked her to marry me once. Not so long ago.

SARA. I should have laughed at all the wrong times.

RUDI. I thought maybe you would, so I gave it up.

[*To* JOHN *again*]:

Now I wish I hadn't. She might not be marrying Clevenger now if . . .

JOHN. He's taking her out of our lives and a great store of our balance and humanity with her.

[SARA *frowns.*]

SARA. At least I'm taking him out of your lives.

JOHN. Only you aren't. We'll never be free of him.

Every day I'll remember how the business was saved.
You'll be running an anti-war paper on war profits.

RUDI.   Well, Nobel earned his peace prize off dynamite.

JOHN.   What's the answer? Or did Martin find the
answer?

RUDI.   He found one answer. Clevenger's got the other.
We haven't got any.

JOHN.   Us liberals!

[*And he shakes his head with melancholy humor.
Then, however, he turns with a new seriousness
to Rudi.*]

Reason, though. And "the good life" and "live and let
live" and "both sides of the question": somebody's got to
worry about 'em! Damn it, Rudi, when the shouting's all
over and done with, whom will they have to clean up the
mess but us liberals?

[*The Scotch mist clears a little for* RUDI.]

RUDI.   Search me!

JOHN.   [*His conviction growing*]: No, I'm serious,
Rudi! Our Yankee ancestors made our kind the guardians
of man's faith in himself! Not in leaders or dogmas or
governments, but himself! That's what we mustn't forget!

RUDI.   I won't forget.

JOHN.   Liberalism: a goal man's never been able to at-
tain, a hope man's never been able to abandon.

RUDI.   Democracy.

[*The word sticks.*]

JOHN.   Don't laugh.

SARA.   He wasn't laughing. That's the White Rock.

RUDI.   Neither Hitler nor Marx. Just . . .

[*With care*]:

Democracy. Foggy or not.

> [*He rises. His stance is none too steady as he moves away from the table.*]

JOHN.   It isn't easy to walk the middle way.

RUDI.   It isn't easy for me to walk at all.

> [*But he turns back to answer* JOHN.]

Oh, I'll stick to the middle! And not only because you can see both sides from the middle. You see further ahead from the middle, too!

JOHN.   And if the time comes that we have to choose . . .

RUDI.   Between standing in line thus . . .

> [*The Nazi salute.*]

Or thus . . .

> [*The Communist salute.*]

JOHN.   We can die, can't we?

RUDI.   Or go to the island of Bali.

> [*Then, the front door buzzer sounding*]:

There's the great lover back.

> [JOHN *rises.*]

No, I'll let him in. I'd like him to see me at my best.

> [*He goes into the hall and towards the front door.*]

JOHN.   Oh, Sara! Sara!

SARA.   What?

JOHN.   Can you build for a better world in irony?

SARA.   Better in irony than in violence.

> [*Then, suddenly, she is on her feet and turned towards the hall door—*JOHN *with her—as the entire house is shattered by the sound of* JOAN's *hysteri-*

cal sobbing. It is the most complete possible let-
ting go of uncontrolled agony. Through it the
*sound of voices—*RUDI's *and* ROGER's—*then* RUDI,
sobered or as good, meets SARA *and* JOHN *in the*
hall.]

RUDI.   Holy God, do you hear that? She's just . . .

[*Then* ROGER *supports his sister to the foot of the*
stair and, almost at once, DORIS *is down to them*
from above and MARY *after her.* MARTIN, *in*
pajamas and bathrobe, an unbecoming plaster
over one ear, trails after them.]

SARA.   Joan! Joan, darling! What is it?

ROGER.   It's Steve! Crashed! Crashed right in front of
her eyes!

SARA.   She wasn't going with him!

ROGER.   We were both going with him!

[*The remainder, of course, comes with a rush.*]

SARA.   Oh, my poor Joan!

ROGER.   Only we got there too late!

[*Together*]

JOHN.   Thank God you did!

DORIS.   Get ice water, Mary! And spirits of ammonia!

[MARY *hurries back up the stair.*]

ROGER.   All the way from the air-port I had that! Driving, too!

[*Together*]

SARA.   There's Doctor Miller just across the street!

JOHN.   What's his telephone number?

RUDI.   The hell with the telephone! I can run across!

[*He goes.*]

SARA.   [*At the same time*]: Try to stop it, Joan! Try! Take hold of yourself! . . .

> [*She has put her arm about her daughter's shoulders. But JOAN shakes loose and things are clear for a moment.*]

JOAN.   Not you! Not you! I don't want you to touch me!

[SARA *recoils involuntarily.*]

It wouldn't have happened if you'd stopped him!

SARA.   [*The deepest distress*]: Joan, darling!

JOAN.   I'd be with him now, if you hadn't stopped me!

[*And she turns into her aunt's arms.*]

Oh, Aunt Doris! Aunt Doris!

DORIS.   Joan, I know! I understand!

JOAN.   It burned him! It burned him!

[*Then confusion again.*]

JOHN.   Get her up to her room!

[*And to* JOAN]:

And lie down on your bed and try to . . .

> [*They are trying to get her up the stair but her collapse on the first step makes things difficult.*]

JOAN.   [*Throughout*]: But Mother stopped me! That's what I can't forget! I could have been with him! I'll never forgive . . .

SARA.   Oh, my poor Joan! My poor Joan!

JOHN.   [*At the same time*]: Now, it's all right, Joan! It's all right!

> [*He is carrying her up,* DORIS *preceding them.* RUDI *returns and with him* DOCTOR MILLER—*any age at all—in the dinner coat of his New Year's party.*]

SARA.   This is very bad, doctor. Thank you for coming over!

DOCTOR MILLER.   Rudi told me. I think we can get her quieted down.

JOAN.   [*At the same time*]: Don't leave me, Aunt Doris!

DORIS.   [*From above*]: I won't, Joan. I'm just . . .

> [*The procession disappears above, leaving* ROGER *and* RUDI *below. A moment more of the sobbing and voices, then everything is shut off as though by the closing of* JOAN'S *bedroom door.*]

ROGER.   What do they do to stop a thing like that?

RUDI.   Opiates, I guess. Put her to sleep.

> [*He comes back into the room.*]

What the hell happened and did she see it happen?

ROGER.   Just as we got there, I tell you!

> [*He comes into the room as* RUDI *proceeds to move the whiskey and White Rock empties to a side table.*]

We got there just as he taxied out into the snow. They'd tried to stop him. I don't believe any one could have stopped him. The snow hid him. God knows what happened then! They guessed he must have skidded on his take-off. We only heard the crash. Then the flames shot up. You couldn't even see them for the snow. A red brightness, that's all. And a roaring that made even the snow feel hot! We saw 'em bring him in on the truck. I couldn't look.

RUDI.   [*Under his breath*]: Holy God!

> [SARA *and* JOHN *are coming back down the stair.*
> *They enter the room.*]

SARA.   [*To* RUDI]: She won't let me near her. Doris is the one she wants with her now. I haven't forgotten how she feels, so thank God for Doris. Somebody give me a cigarette.

JOHN.   How about a spot of brandy?

SARA.   Just a cigarette.

> [JOHN *is delivering. She sees* MARTIN.]

Martin!

> [*None of the others had noticed his presence. Now*
> *they all realize the blow he has sustained.* SARA
> *goes to him but can think of nothing to say and*
> *merely touches his arm with her own warm sym-*
> *pathy. Then*]:

You should be in bed.

MARTIN.   I'm all right.

> [*Then*]:

Who would have thought our sedate little Joan could have had a mess like this in store for her?

> [*Then*]:

You don't have to have me on your minds!

[*Then*]:

All war seems to have got itself crammed into these few hours. The hero and the dissenter both picked off. And each in the way most suitable to him.

[*Then*]:

Well, good night.

[*He goes up the stair again.*]

SARA. It's hard to know what to do. I ought to be out at that airport now!

JOHN. Sara, what for?

SARA. Jim must be out there!

ROGER. He is.

SARA. I can't leave him alone out there with that . . .

[*She stops herself, then*]:

Rudi, as soon as the doctor says Joan's all right, I'll ask you to take me . . .

> [*The doorbell. A pause.* JOHN *goes. Then* CLEV-ENGER *appears in the hall. He moves heavily, a man still groggy from the impact of horror.* OCKLEFORD *joins him to help him off with his coat.* JOHN *comes last.*]

CLEVENGER. [*Orders, but effort behind every word of them*]: You'd better get on the phone to *The Eagle*. Warn 'em against giving the accident too much space. The fact of its having occurred at the local airport is not—I'm most particular about this—to interfere with the National

Honor campaign. Make sure the railroad has a car for me on that nine-whatever-it-is out of here in the morning.

> [*He comes into the room as* OCKLEFORD *goes. He is darkly but fully possessed of himself. He looks about him.* SARA's *eyes are downcast. Likewise* RUDI's. JOHN *waits in the hall. It is* ROGER *who steps impetuously into the silence.*]

ROGER.   I want to tell you I'm sorry, sir. Steve Andrews was just God Almighty to me!

> [*He goes out and up the stair.* CLEVENGER *turns to the brothers.*]

CLEVENGER.   If you're reading some damn pacifist lesson into what's happened, there's none to be read! The boy himself was to blame! He had no business trying to get to France! None flying in this weather!

> [*A gesture from* SARA, *and* RUDI *goes into the parlor, closing the door after him.* JOHN *likewise closes the hall door.*]

Thank you.

SARA.   Flying in the air over the earth—that's an unreal and unhuman thing, isn't it? Even death from flying doesn't seem like death.

CLEVENGER.   It's the earth taking its own back.

SARA.   If I can do anything that will help at all . . . What do you want me to do?

> [*A look at her and he goes to sit down.*]

CLEVENGER.   I think you know that.

> [SARA *is distressed.*]

SARA. I couldn't very well leave Joan now, could I?

CLEVENGER. How quickly can you come to me, Sara? If I can know that—just that, just a date . . .

SARA. [*A plea*]: Don't try to pin me down!

CLEVENGER. Sara, you're not . . .?

[*He darts a sharp look of suspicion at her, then*]:

No, you couldn't do that to me now!

[*But* SARA *cries out, almost in physical pain.*]

SARA. Oh, please! I'm tired.

CLEVENGER. I don't mean to press you. But I'm afraid to be alone . . . with that poor burned body.

[SARA's *eyes close to shut out the picture.*]

SARA. Try not to think about that.

CLEVENGER. I'll always reproach myself. I said things to him that I'll always be sorry for.

SARA. Better not think about that either.

CLEVENGER. They tell me people get over blows like this. But I've nothing left now that I've lost the boy. You see that, don't you?

[*She looks away.*]

SARA. Yes. Oh, yes. I see.

CLEVENGER. You, only you, can heal me and fill my loneliness! Pity me, Sara! Pity my loneliness!

SARA. [*The deepest conceivable unhappiness*]: I pity you, Jim! I do pity you!

CLEVENGER. Then you'll come with me tomorrow, won't you? The boy's death in those flames must have sealed things for us! And we'll take him to Washington together! To Arlington! They wanted to bury him here on the field where he fell, but we'll bury him there with full military honors!

[*His head is up and his eyes are blazing.*]

I shall acknowledge him to the world as my son now, Sara! I don't have to say he was rushing to fly with the French. Let 'em think he was on his way to offer his life for his own country! That way they'll never forget him! I'll keep his name alive to the day of my death! Steve Andrews who was really Steve Clevenger! The greatest flyer of all time and my son! My son and the first hero of the new war!

[*This is much too much for* Sara, *but he notices nothing.*]

Ockleford! Ockleford!

Sara. [*Low*]: Don't, Jim! Please don't!

[Ockleford *returns from the hall.*]

Clevenger. Get on the phone to *The Eagle!* Stop the presses! Tell 'em I'm coming down to tear the front page wide open!

[Ockleford *goes.*]

I've found how to tie Steve's death in with National Honor! I'll get out a memorial edition of every damn one of my papers and acknowledge the boy in facsimile of my own hand-writing spread all over every front page! By God, Sara, I'll . . .

[*But all this is now far too much for* Sara.]

Sara. Of course you don't have to think such things out! You do them by instinct, don't you?

CLEVENGER.   Now what do you mean by that?

SARA.   Your instinct to use everything, even that poor, burned body, to your advantage.

> [*He lurches angrily at her, but her steadiness holds him.*]

CLEVENGER.   I hope you may some day forgive yourself for saying that!

> [SARA *shakes her head.*]

SARA.   I shall have forgotten tomorrow that I said it. It's odd that I should have let you use what you have used this week and made excuses for you and that I should stick now on this!

> [*He goes to her, shaking with fury.*]

CLEVENGER.   You make me wish we hadn't met again and that this past week had never been!

> [*But* SARA *is equal to him.*]

SARA.   Your week hasn't been wasted! You've done what you had to do supremely well! You found us a family unafraid even of the disaster you saved us from! You'll leave us a zoo of prosperous lost souls! Twenty years of my dreams were invested here! Well, you've brought my investment off bankrupt! You've made shoddy melodrama of my daughter's life and given my son a mission of destruction! And all that's only incidental, I know! You'll go on! There's no one with the strength or vision to stop you! But you can't ask me to compromise with you now! Those who've nothing to offer can't compromise! And you've left me in command of a total wreck!

> [*And she calls*]:

Rudi! John!

> [*But* RUDI *and* JOHN, *alarmed by the clamor of her outburst, are already standing at the parlor door.*]

It's all right! I only wanted the interruption!

> [CLEVENGER *does not welcome the interruption, but he manages to laugh it off pleasantly.*]

RUDI.   I didn't hear anything funny.

CLEVENGER.   I know how you both feel but I don't give her up. And she won't be such a fool as to let me go. These are my times! That's my star up there!

SARA.   What does a woman do, under your star, who can't look at life from your side of the river?

CLEVENGER.   One thing you three will come to realize some day: that my creed holds water for the world we live in. I can't see that yours holds water even for you.

> [OCKLEFORD *has come into the hall for* CLEVENGER'S *hat and coat.*]

OCKLEFORD.   Ready to go down to *The Eagle*, Chief?

CLEVENGER.   I think so.

> [*With the best of good humor, he drops an affectionate arm around* SARA'S *shoulders. She looks up at him.*]

SARA.   Take care you don't catch another stiff neck.

> [*He frowns because he does not like jokes at the expense of his health. But he is too surely in command of things to let* SARA *feel his annoyance.*]

CLEVENGER.   You'll still be up when I get back. You've got packing to do.

> [*A final affectionate pat and he goes out towards the front door*, OCKLEFORD *following with the hat and coat.*]

JOHN.   He doesn't realize he's out.

RUDI.   [*Quickly*]: He *is* out?

SARA.   Twenty years ago I loved him and told him he wasn't good enough to love. Now I've loved him again and can find nothing better to say about him. That's a little sad.

> [*She smiles.*]

It's sad, too, for a woman to hear the last call from the dining car—and pass it up.

RUDI.   I can see that.

> [*He sits timidly, as it seems, not knowing what to say next.* JOHN, *too, is silent and ill at ease.*]

SARA.   [*To* RUDI]: Don't let it depress you.

> [*Then*]:

Is there any more coffee in this thing?

> [*She sits and refills her cup.*]

RUDI.   [*To* JOHN]: Remember how they used to give us our supper in here after mother died? And the old man sitting there in that chair of Sara's glaring at us?

JOHN.   How often we three have sat here like this!

SARA.   Where were we ten years ago, before Joan came home?

> [JOHN *sits.*]

JOHN.   Discussing the irony of our predicament.

RUDI.   So we were!

SARA.   And I was about to say that it doesn't matter.

JOHN.   I'd like to know what does!

[*Her strength is returning to her.*]

SARA.   I can't tell you that. But I can't feel too sorry for you! Oh, I know he's confused you now and set you back! But I read in a book once: "Stone the idealist—no flint can reach his thought. Bury the dreamer—his dreams will color the sky above his grave. Imprison the philosopher—his philosophy will wander free in the market place."

[*From far away the* HORNS *and* SIRENS *welcome in the New Year.*]

Listen! Happy New Year!

[RUDI *rises and* JOHN *sits up, both in protest.*]

Oh, not this year or next, I grant you. Or, perhaps, any that we shall ever see. Some year, though . . . Some year . . .

[*The* HORNS *continue. She sips her coffee. The curtain falls.*]

THE END

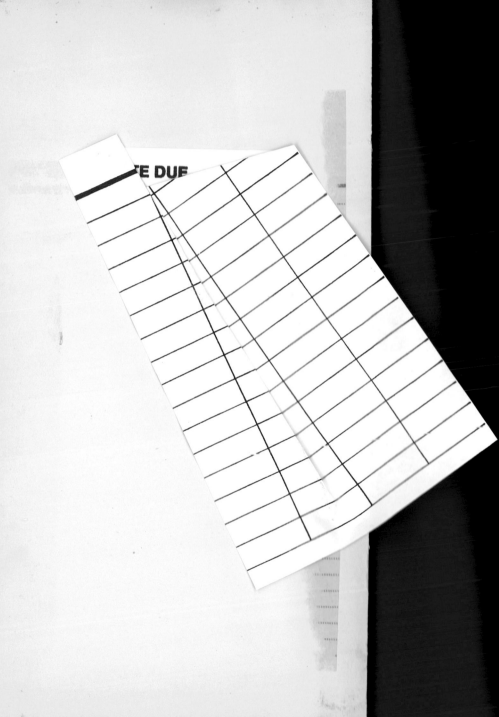

DATE DUE